AF588466

THE TEQUILA BIBLE

INCLUDES 20
COCKTAIL RECIPES

THE TEQUILA BIBLE

The complete lowdown on the spirit—more than 200 tequilas tried & tested

ERIC ZANDONA

MITCHELL
BEAZLEY

CONTENTS

Introduction 6

PART 1: **The Basics** 8

A Quick History of Tequila 10

How Tequila is Made 34

How to Read a Tequila Label 52

PART 2: **The Tequilas** 60

PART 3: **The Cocktails** 172

Short Drinks 176

Drinks Served Up 188

Tall Drinks 202

Glossary 216

Index 218

Picture Credits 222

Acknowledgements 223

In the two decades since 2005, sales of tequila have grown at a meteoric rate, outpacing almost all other major categories of spirits. In 2023, for the first time ever, US consumers purchased more tequila than American whiskey, making it the second-largest spirit category after vodka. Tequila's popularity isn't just limited to North America; it is also one of the fastest-growing spirit categories in the UK and Europe.

Introduction

Much of this growth can be credited to a radical change in consumer perception of tequila from a cheap party drink full of bad memories to an artisanal, aspirational, and authentic spirit full of history and romance.

One driver of this change in attitude is tequila's ability to innovate and simultaneously appeal to an increasingly fragmented consumer base. With more than 2,000 brands on the market, tequila has the uncanny ability to sincerely reflect the values and aspirations of the consumers back to them. There are legacy brands, celebrity brands, women-owned brands, kosher brands, and organic brands; brands for the nightclub, brands for purists, brands for whiskey drinkers, and brands for vodka drinkers; brands for mixing, brands for sipping, and brands for craft cocktails. Whatever you are looking for, there is a tequila brand for you.

As tequila is native to Mexico, much of the language that describes the spirit—including how it is made and the plant that is made from—is based in Spanish and various indigenous languages. This can create a barrier for those who are just getting into this incredible spirit. To overcome this, *The Tequila Bible* is written as a guide for the tequila curious, new devotees, and seasoned fans alike. The opening section

ABOVE Blue agave—the starting point for all tequila.

offers a solid foundation for understanding the historical, cultural, and technical developments of the spirit. This is followed with a description of the unique morphology of the blue agave, a primer on how tequila is made and where its flavors come from. This section closes with a chapter on how to decode the language and terminology found on a tequila label.

The main section of the book is designed to help you discover your new favorite tequila (or five), to inspire, and to aid the discovery of what flavors you like best and where they come from. Every tequila expression includes background information on the brand and a thorough taste profile, as well as a quick key with information on where and how the tequila is made. Use this section to discover the tequilas you enjoy most, which have similar flavor profiles to those you already like, and to identify which you should try next. The final section offers 20 suggested cocktails designed to bring out the best features of tequila. They have also been selected to illustrate that tequila cocktails can pair perfectly with any mood or drinking occasion.

I hope *The Tequila Bible* will challenge common misconceptions about tequila, as well as your preconceived notions about particular brands or styles; and persuade you to adopt my belief that the subjective experience of flavor—not price, popularity, or rarity—is the most important factor. Whatever type of tequila you enjoy, use this book to guide you through the wonderful world of flavors waiting to be explored.

Peñol dl teul
P. dl mizton
Teçoles de gra
teqla
yçatla
cuyupuytlan
Cuidad de gua
dalajara
minas ó plata
Ameca

ORDINARIO

THE BASICS

1

A Quick History of Tequila

The story of tequila begins with the merging of cultures and people during the Spanish Conquest of the Aztec Empire. In 1519, when Hernán Cortés and his conquistadors landed in what is now modern Mexico they encountered people who had more than 10,000 years of experience and a culture tied to a family of succulent plants we know now as agave (ug-gah-vey). As the Spanish colonized Mexico, they found different groups of people using different species of agaves for similar needs. In central Mexico, the Aztecs and others used some species of the succulent for food while others collected and fermented raw agave sap to create a nutritious and lightly alcoholic drink called pulque (pull-kay). There is evidence that in western Mexico people used cooked agave for both food and to make alcohol. The Spanish documented some of these indigenous traditions and practices but, according to these records, none of them practiced distilling.

The Many Names for Agave

When you read historic accounts of Mexico between the 1500–1700s, you'll notice that there are several different words that point to agave plants. Part of the reason for this is that the Spanish, who hadn't encountered the plant until their arrival in the New World, relied on local names for the plant which they then adopted and translated into the Spanish language. Their first encounter with agave was in the Caribbean. The Taíno people, who inhabited many of the islands, had a name for the agave which the Spanish wrote down as "maguey". When the Spanish landed in Mexico, they found plants that looked like those they'd seen on the Caribbean islands—so they called them magueys even though the local people used different names. When the Spanish asked what words were used for maguey, they recorded mexcatl, or mezcalí, which later morphed into the modern word mezcal. Ironically, these words were not the name of the plant, but words for cooked agave. Over time, the Spanish settled on maguey for the plant and mezcal for the spirit made from cooked maguey. Outside of Mexico, Swedish botanist Carl Linnaeus listed magueys in his book *Species Plantarum* (1753) under the scientific name "agave", which was translated from the Greek word "agauós", which means noble. In 1797, a definition for agave described the plant as an American aloe, which became commonly used in the US.

Distilling technology was independently invented a couple of times around the world, though most civilizations learned the technology from someone else. It is certain, however, that the people in China and Mesopotamia invented their own distinct distilling technologies. China's distilling process spread throughout Asia to the Philippines islands, and was adapted by people along the way, while the distilling technology from the Muslim world expanded west into Europe. In the 8th century, Abū Mūsā Jābir ibn Hayyān, a Muslim alchemist, improved on the distilling technology with the invention of the alembic pot still. The Muslims introduced distilling to the Spanish during the 700-year Muslim occupation of the Iberian Peninsula from 711–1492.

ABOVE Abū Mūsā Jābir ibn Hayyān, inventor of the alembic pot still.

LEFT Spanish conquistador, Hernán Cortés, with Aztec rulers in the early 16th century.

From the 1520s to the 1580s, the Spanish and Filipinos both brought their distilling technologies and traditions to Mexico, where they began making spirits from back home. The Spanish used their alembic still to make brandy within a few years of the arrival of wine grapes in 1524. Similarly, Filipinos began making spirits from fermented coconut using their own traditional still design. In the Philippines, this spirit is known as lambanóg (lam-ba-nog) but in Mexico it became known as "vino de coco" (coconut wine). Coconuts were brought to

ABOVE Don Pedro Sánchez de Tagle, often misinterpreted as the "Father of Tequila."

modern-day Colima in Mexico in 1569 and, within a couple of decades, thousands of liters of vino de coco were being distilled every year using Filipino-style stills made from a hollowed-out tree trunk and a copper bowl full of cold water. But the central question is: when did Mexicans begin distilling agave?

If you were to search for the person who invented tequila you would most likely come across Don Pedro Sánchez de Tagle and the claim that he is the "Father of Tequila." As the story goes, Don Pedro purchased an estate called Hacienda Cuisillos near the current day town of Tequila, where he began distilling agave spirits in the year 1600. At first glance, the story appears to be true: Don Pedro was a real person and Hacienda Cuisillos was a real place. However, when you scrutinize the details, the tale quickly falls apart. First, Don Pedro Sánchez de Tagle was born in Spain in 1661—it is impossible for him to have invented tequila 61 years earlier. Second, he did not

The Mythological Origins of Agave

In Aztec mythology, the feathered serpent god Quetzalcóatl (ket-suhl-Ko-Waa-tl) went on a journey searching the universe for something he could give to mankind to bring them joy. As he searched, he found the beautiful goddess Mayahuel (My-ya-whel) who was being held captive by her jealous grandmother Tzitzimitl (TSEET-TSEE-mi-tl) in the realm of the celestial demons. Quetzalcóatl freed Mayahuel and they escaped to earth and hid together in the form of a tree. When Tzitzimitl discovered their disguise, her demons tore Quetzalcóatl and Mayahuel apart and devoured Mayahuel's body. In grief, Quetzalcóatl buried the remains of Mayahuel in the earth. Out of her grave grew the first agave, from which humanity received food, clothing, soap, shelter, and a fermented drink that brought joy to mankind.

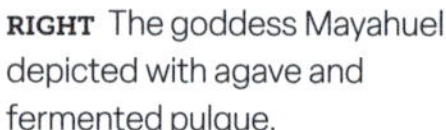

RIGHT The goddess Mayahuel depicted with agave and fermented pulque.

ABOVE 16th-century map of Nueva Galicia.

purchase Hacienda Cuisillos until 1702. And third, official records of Hacienda Cuisillos do not list a distillery as present on the property: when Don Pedro purchased the Hacienda, and later when it became part of a dowry for one of his heirs, there was an accounting of its total acreage, the number of livestock, buildings on the land, and even the value of the furniture—but neither document lists a distillery.

Setting Don Pedro aside, there is evidence that agave spirits—and what we would later come to know as tequila—most likely originate in Nueva Galicia and were born sometime in the first 20 years of the 17th century. Nueva Galicia was an administrative region that covered parts of the modern-day Mexican States of Aguascalientes, Guanajuato, Colima, Jalisco, Nayarit, and Zacatecas. In 1580 a report was written for King Philip II of Spain, called *Relaciones Geográficas de Nueva Galicia*, that described the many uses the native peoples had for the agave plant. The author noted that different communities used agaves (called both mexcatl and magueys in the report) for making "wine, vinegar, honey, string, rope, wood for houses, needles, nails, thread, [and] balsam for injuries." From this context, the wine referred to was most likely the fermented juice extracted from cooked agaves. By 1621, however, wine made from agaves—or vino de mezcal—came to refer to a spirit distilled from cooked agaves. Domingo Lázaro de Arregui

ABOVE Botanical illustration of the agave plant from 1886.

recorded in this book, *Descripción de la Nueva Galicia*, how the locals made wine that was "clearer than water and stronger than aguardiente (another Spanish word for distilled spirits), and has a similar flavor." According to Lázaro de Arregui, the roots and stems of the agave plant were roasted, squeezed to extract a must, fermented, and then distilled. Two years later in 1623, Fray Antonio de Tello traveled these same regions and described the stills that locals used to make these vinos. "The stills are hollow trunks, the thickness of a man, covered by a copper encasing full of water." Throughout the rest of the century, there were multiple independent reports from travelers in Jalisco and Colima that described how local people had adopted the Filipino style still of making spirits from cooked agave.

From Vino de Mezcal to Tequila

Over the 200-year period from 1595 to 1795, the Spanish Crown went through periods of loosely enforced prohibition. In 1595, King Philip II of Spain banned the planting of new vineyards in Mexico, restricting local production to increase demand for Spanish wine and brandy in the New World. This prohibition had limited success. The Catholic Church retained the ability to create sacramental wine, meaning commercial wine production did not stop in Mexico, rather it moved from lands controlled by noble families to lands controlled by the Church. During the 17th century, vast mining operations were set up throughout Mexico. Mexican mines were notorious for their harsh conditions and many of their workers turned to drink for comfort. Early on, miners relied on vino de coco, but over successive prohibition efforts in 1595, 1603, and 1610, production was squeezed and vino de mezcal began to fill in the gaps. By the beginning of the 1700s, vino de coco was largely wiped out partially because its production relied on being located near to large coconut plantations. In contrast, distillers of vino de mezcal began to thrive partly because they were spread out across the countryside and operated clandestinely. One of the challenges for Spanish prohibition was Mexican governors, who were supposed to enforce the laws but were simultaneously collecting tax revenue from alcohol's production.

Most histories of tequila incorrectly begin with King Ferdinand VI of Spain granting José Antonio de Cuervo y Valdés land outside the town of Tequila in 1758. Instead, historical record shows that José Antonio purchased land being auctioned by The Office of Bishop José Reyes Gómez de Aguilar in 1758, when he took possession of the land acting as the "steward" of The Brotherhood of the Blessed Souls of Purgatory of Tequila organization. The Brotherhood was chartered by the Catholic Church to raise funds for the

LEFT José Antonio de Cuervo, "steward" of land in Tequila where the production of tequila spirit began.

construction of a church in Tequila, pay for church services for members who had passed away, provide food to the needy, and help the souls of those who died in Tequila get out of purgatory. The Brotherhood held land on behalf of its members, who continued to earn an income from it while also using some of the proceeds to fund their charitable works. As steward, José Antonio was responsible for managing the Brotherhood's assets, as well as leasing out the land to farmers and distillers.

After José Antonio's death around 1764, his sons José Prudencio de Cuervo y Montaño and José María Guadalupe de Cuervo y Montaño continued the legacy he'd begun. Both sons served as stewards of the Brotherhood and they continued to oversee the growth of sugar cane and agaves, as well as the distillation of vino de mezcal on their lands. In 1785, King Charles III of Spain outlawed the production of Mexican-made alcohol to increase demand for Spanish wine and brandy once again. However, records show that both José Prudencio and José María continued to grow and sell agaves, which were likely turned into vino de mezcal. Fortunately for the Cuervo family, this prohibition was short lived. Charles III died in 1788 and his son Charles IV ascended to the throne. In 1795, Charles IV lifted the ban on the production of Mexican alcohol and José María Cuervo received the first license in Tequila to officially produce vino de mezcal at his taberna de Cuervo (Cuervo Distillery).

During the next century, Mexico experienced a series of hardships: between 1810 and 1867, Mexico fought a war of independence from Spain, faced a revolt in Texas, fought two wars with France, endured two major earthquakes, and was invaded by the United States resulting in the loss of territory from Alta California to New Mexico. All the while, Tequila's vinos de mezcal slowly gained notoriety and became known simply as mezcal de Tequila. But the Cuervo family also went through a period of ups and downs. By December 1811, both José Prudencio and José Maria had died, and the ownership of their lands had passed to María Magdalena Cuervo Carrillo, José Maria's daughter. The following year, María Magdalena married Vicente Albino Rojas Jiménez and control of the land and distillery moved to her new husband. Vicente Albino renamed the Taberna de Cuervo after himself, changing the name to La Rojeña, which remains its name today.

La Rojeña flourished under Vicente Albino and production grew. By the middle of the century, the distillery was producing hundreds of barrels a week and was reported to have more than three million agave plants in the ground. After Vicente Albino's death in 1868, his daughters handed control of La

BELOW Chopping piñas at La Rojeña distillery.

Rojeña and its assets to another successful distiller named Jesús Flores y Ponce. Jesús Flores owned two other distilleries, La Floreña and La Constancia.

It was during this era that tequila began to distinguish itself from other mezcals. In 1854, a Frenchman named Ernest Vigneaux remarked that: "Tequila lends its name to the mezcal liquor, in the same way Cognac does to the liquors of France." But what was it about tequila that made it stand out in this way? During the first 200 years of vino de mezcal, very little had changed in how it was distilled. Mature agaves were harvested, roasted in earthen pits, crushed by hand, fermented in wooden vats, and distilled in Filipino-style stills. But by the time of José María Guadalupe de Cuervo, the process had most likely transitioned to include permanent stone-lined pits for roasting, mule drawn tahonas (mill stones), and wood-fired copper alembic stills. It is probable that some of these small changes helped to refine the flavor and quality of tequila and explain why it began to stand out from the rest.

The major change for mezcal de Tequila came in the second half of the 19th century, when distillers in and around Tequila transitioned from pit-roasting agaves to cooking them in above-ground brick ovens. These ovens required less wood to heat and, as a result, they imparted less wood smoke into the spirit, which the public enjoyed. By the end of the century, the largest distillers in Tequila had transitioned to steam power, both for cooking and distilling. This removed any vestiges of smoke from the spirit and marked the dividing line between mezcal de Tequila and the modern-day spirit. While distillers continued to use vino de mezcal and mezcal de Tequila on their labels for the next few decades, the spirit had become something new.

Sharing Tequila with the World

Until the mid-1850s tequila was almost exclusively consumed in Mexico, but by the time the first barrels reached the United States, it was clearly distinguished from other types of mezcal. On July 22 1852, Thomas Beale & Co. placed an advertisement in the Daily Alta California newspaper that they had 1000 gallons of legitimate mezcal de Tequila that had just arrived from the port of San Blas (today in Nayarit) for sale at the Sacramento street wharf in San Francisco. The ad does not say where the tequila came from but it aligns with Casa Cuervo's claim that they were the first to export barrels of tequila to California via San Blas. However, for the next few years there were no new shipments advertised. Through the early 1870s there were sporadic mentions of tequila outside of Mexico, but by the middle of that decade advertisements for tequila became more frequent.

It seems that one of the driving forces that helped push tequila to a wider audience was the rivalry between Jesue

ABOVE Tequila's expansion into international markets began at the Chicago World's Fair in 1893.

Flores and former employee turned distillery owner, Cenobio Sauza. Distillers in Tequila, including Flores and Sauza, began selling their spirits in 5-liter glass bottles called demijohns in part because they were easier than barrels for untrained freight workers to transport. As glass technology advanced, both companies invested in factories to bring their spirits to more people. By 1910, several tequila distillers had begun selling their spirits in small "pachoncita" bottles of about 500ml. However, shipping tequila in bottles or barrels to faraway destinations like the United States was costly. Because of this, Sauza and Flores temporarily put their rivalry aside to persuade the Mexican government of the urgent need for railroads connecting Jalisco and the US. Their cooperation in this area paid off and by 1888, there were rail lines connecting Guadalajara to El Paso, Texas via Mexico City.

With the packaging and transportation issues solved, tequila needed a way to attract more customers. Distillers used a series of world fairs and competitions to help grow the profile of the spirit. These events also made it possible for people around the world to taste and learn about tequila for the first time. This began with the Chicago World's Fair in 1893, where mezcal de Tequila famously brought home a gold medal. Newspapers from this time inform their readers that, when looking for this "Mexican brandy", they should only look for authentic "mezcal de Tequila". Tequilas made by Cuervo, Sauza, and others had similar results at the 1904 World's Fair in St. Louis, Missouri. Internationally, Jose Cuervo Tequila won awards in a series of competitions held at racing events including the 1907 Gran Premio in Madrid, Spain, and at the 1909 Grand Prix in Paris, France. These events helped position tequila in the same conversations as other world class drinks such as brandy, whiskey, gin, and champagne.

Tequila's 40-Year Economic Rollercoaster

Over the 40-year period from 1910 to 1950 tequila went through a series of busts and booms that changed the spirit forever. From 1910 to 1920, the Mexican Revolution upended the political and economic life of the country. In Jalisco, revolutionaries confiscated tequila, destroyed rail lines, and attempts at land reform broke up some of the existing distillery estates. As the revolution came to an end, the US was beginning its "noble experiment" with prohibition. Mexican distillers took the opportunity to make some much-needed sales by delivering tequila to rum runners and bootleggers, who then moved it across the border. But this too was short-lived. By 1929, only eight large distilleries continued making tequila and the Great Depression that began in the US reverberated across Mexico. Decreased demand for tequila caused farmers to abandon their agave plants in favor of other more profitable crops. Because of this, there was a significant shortage of agaves by the 1930s and, in a devil's bargain, some distillers started making tequila with sugar cane. A few began adding cane sugar directly into fermenters to keep up with demand, while others lengthened the supply of the tequila on

LEFT Francisco "Pancho" Villa, general in the Mexican Revolution.

RIGHT Separating agave fibers at the Jose Cuervo distillery.

hand with the addition of cane spirit (rum). It was also during this period that the Tequila Herradura brand began differentiating itself by labeling its tequila as being made with 100% agave. Then, as the US entered World War II, demand for tequila shot up as US distillers transitioned their production capacity to the war effort. This increase in demand caused new agave plantings to double every year for the rest of the war. However, as blue agaves can take eight or more years to fully grow, there was a lag in the supply of mature plants. For this—and other economic—reasons, many brands continued making tequila throughout the war and into peacetime with agave and cane sugar. Once the war ended, so did rationing, and US distillers moved quickly to slake the thirst of returning vets. This dried up the demand for tequila just as millions of agaves came close to maturity and harvesting.

Defining Tequila

In 1947, the Mexican government and the tequila industry saw the handwriting on the wall with the coming wave of mature agave. If the industry continued to make tequila with other sugars, the price of agave would fall below subsistence level for many farmers. It was feared that this would create a feedback loop where farmers would rip out agaves for annual crops, which would lead to an insufficient supply and cause prices for agave to explode thereby bringing in a flood of farmers planting new agave. To avoid this cycle and repair tequila's damaged reputation from years of substandard spirits, the industry and government agreed to create a set of legal standards for the spirit.

Mexico began by passing a series of laws defining tequila that, on their surface, were about protecting the quality of the spirit. The Mexican government passed the first law (DGN. R9-1949) on 12 May 1949—and by today's standards it set a high bar for production. Tequila was defined as type of mezcal obtained from the blue agave and other agaves grown in Jalisco. The agaves had to be cooked, crushed, fermented, distilled once with bagazo (agave fibers), and a second time to increase its strength. It could be bottled unaged or aged between 45 and 50% ABV. If the tequila was aged, it had to spend a minimum of two years in oak barrels. Interestingly, the law specified that unaged tequila, what it called "Tequila Natural", could not have any added sugar but añejo (aged) tequilas could contain up to 5.4g of added sugar per liter.

One criticism of the laws defining tequila is that they have just codified what the largest distillers want or need at any given moment in time instead of focusing on the quality of tequila or protecting a narrowly defined regional spirit. In the 1950s, the post-war boom hit Mexico and demand for tequila once again outpaced the supply of agave and, within a decade the industry was facing another shortage. Distillers and the government returned to the idea of increasing the supply of tequila by supplementing it with cane sugar. But, to do so, they would need to amend the existing law. While the 1949 law allowed the use of other agaves in tequila production, the industry had become so entwined with the blue agave that there was no thought to allow other agave species from outside of Jalisco to supplement future shortages. Instead, the 1964 update stipulated that tequila could only be made with blue agave grown in Jalisco and be supplemented with no more than 30% of other non-agave sugars. If a distiller chose to supplement their blue agave with other sugars, though, they did not have to say anything on the label—it would continue to be tequila.

This change codified what the industry had practiced throughout the 1930s and made tequila completely unique in the spirits world. Whiskey, brandy, rum, and tequila had all been defined by their agricultural source: whiskey could only be made with grains, brandy with fruit, rum with sugar cane, and tequila with agave. But, from 1964 on, tequila could also be a hybrid spirit made from agave and sugar cane, and eventfully corn syrup.

The Challenges of Success

From the 1960s on, the US became tequila's largest market and the industry experienced steady growth driven by two key cocktails and a generational change in American drinking preferences. In the 1930s, experienced barmen in the US and Europe discovered that tequila worked particularly well in a daisy cocktail—a style of cocktail with a mix of base spirit, citrus

RIGHT Advertising Jose Cuervo tequila in the USA, 1960s.

juice, sweetener, and orange liqueur. One of the first tequila daisies was the Picador (*see* p. 190), created in 1937 by William J. Tarling, the head bartender at London's Café Royal (*see* pp. 176, 190 and 200) and author of the *Café Royal Cocktail Book*. The following year, another bartender created a similar cocktail based on the combination of tequila, lime, and orange liqueur. This cocktail was named Margarita (*see* p. 176), which could have been named for a woman, but more likely was chosen because "margarita" is the Spanish word for daisy. In 1953, *Esquire* magazine printed a recipe for the Margarita and the Jose Cuervo brand jumped at the opportunity this created. Tequila brands began printing the recipe for a Margarita on their advertisements and tequila house Jose Cuervo even put it on its back label. This tasty cocktail quickly caught on and it drove more people to US liquor stores to pick a bottle of tequila. As this was happening, a new generation of drinkers in the US were moving away from what their parents drank to find something new. Vodka was the big winner in this shift and its sales quickly surpassed whiskey, but tequila became a popular alternative for those that came of age amid the Cold War. In the early 1970s, the Margarita was joined by two new cocktails: Frozen Margarita (*see* p. 188) and Tequila Sunrise (*see* p. 206). In 1971, a Mexican restaurant in Dallas, Texas, began selling hundreds of Frozen Margaritas every night and this boozy, sweet and sour slushy drink spread like wildfire. The following year, the Rolling Stones were introduced to the Tequila Sunrise at a bar outside San Francisco. They loved the drink so much they drank it everywhere they went on the remainder of their 1972 American Tour—or as Keith Richards called it their "Cocaine and Tequila Sunrise" tour. The cocktail quickly caught on and in 1973 the Tequila Sunrise was immortalized in a song by the Eagles.

The popularity of these drinks drove sales of tequila higher and higher, which meant distillers needed more plants in the ground and the spirit would need protection from copycats. In 1968, the definition of tequila was updated to expand the boundaries of where blue agave could be harvested to include Jalisco and areas of "neighboring states" that had similar ecologically characteristics. Two years later, the law was updated again to increase the allowable use of other sugars to 49%. To address the copycat issue, Mexico joined the Lisbon Agreement for the Protection of Appellations of Origin in 1966. This gave Mexico a legally enforceable trademark on the word "tequila," among the other signatory countries. However,

BELOW Blue agave growing in Michoacán state.

ABOVE La Gonzaleña distillery in Tamaulipas.

Mexico did not create its first appellations of origin (Denominación de origen, or DO, in Spanish) until 1974 after Tequila Herradura, The Regional Chamber of Tequila, and The Specialized Agricultural Association of Agave Tequilana Weber Products of Southern Tamaulipas petitioned for its creation.

The 1974 Denomination of Origin for tequila declared it to be a unique product of Mexico, kept most of the 1970 production standards in place and defined the borders of the DO to include Jalisco and select municipalities in Nayarit, Guanajuato, and Michoacán. Interestingly, even though Tamaulipas, which is across the country on the Gulf of Mexico, petitioned to be included in the DO, the government rejected its application as there was no "industrial production" there of a spirit called tequila—despite having plantations full of blue agave.

The obvious question is why was Tamaulipas growing large numbers of blue agave, which were not native to that part of Mexico? In the late 1960s, Francisco Javier Sauza flirted with the idea of building a distillery in Tamaulipas, which would shorten the distance to his largest market in the US. Aware of these plans, Guillermo González Díaz Lombardo began planting blue agave on his large landholdings in Tamaulipas and other farmers followed suit. As the first agaves in Tamaulipas were close to harvest, González learned that Sauza intended to pay below market rate for his agaves. González sought the advice of Guillermo Romo, owner of Tequila Herradura. Romo recommended González use the Herradura engineer to build a distillery in Tamaulipas to make his own tequila.

By 1974, La Gonzaleña distillery was ready to start producing tequila but the government excluded it from the new DO. For two years, González used his political connections in Mexico City to petition the government to allow Tamaulipas to produce and sell tequila. In addition to being a wealthy landowner, González was also a descendant of a former Mexican president. His persistence paid off. In 1976, the newly elected Mexican president brought González together with the other leaders of the tequila industry to resolve the issue. When the government published its updated DO, it said that because "industrialists" in Jalisco induced Tamaulipas to grow blue agave to the tequila industry's standards, the region would be added to the DO. So, in the end, González was successful and 11 municipalities within Tamaulipas were added to the Denomination of Tequila.

One of the issues that the Tamaulipas drama illustrated was that no one was really watching over the industry to enforce the DO and the specifications for making tequila. In 1994, the government wrote a new law (Norma Oficial Mexicana NOM-006-SCFI-1994) defining tequila production and handed responsibility for enforcing the DO and the NOM to a newly created non-profit civil organization— Consejo Regulador Del Tequila (CRT)—which would physically inspect and certify every distillery and brand that sold tequila. The NOM also required distilleries to print their NOM registration number on every label of tequila they produced. In addition, it redefined tequila into two categories and four separate classes. There was "Tequila" for anything made with less than 100% agave, and "100% Agave Tequila". Unaged tequila was named blanco, while joven or gold referred to blanco tequila with added mellowing agents (abocantes). Reposado was tequila aged for a minimum of two months in oak, and añejo for any tequila aged a year or

LEFT Tequilas on sale in the USA in 2025.

more in small oak barrels (maximum 600 l/158 US gallons). For the first time, the NOM defined what abocantes (ah-bow-con-tez) distillers could use to soften and enhance the color, flavor, and texture of their spirits. These included caramel coloring, natural oak extract, glycerin, and sugar syrups. It's likely that these were already widely used before the law was updated and codified their use. The NOM specified that distillers could only use abocantes in joven, reposado, or añejo tequilas; and, in lab analysis there could be no more than 5g/liter of dry solids (abocantes) in the tequila.

One problem with Tequila's Denomination of Origin was that neither the US nor Canada formally recognized Mexico's trademark for tequila. The US and Canada were not a signatory of the Lisbon Agreement so they had no obligation to recognize tequila as a unique product of Mexico. In 1988, Mexico approached the US to create a free trade agreement like the one the US had with Canada. Canada became concerned that Mexico would undercut its trade with the US, so the three countries began negotiating a trilateral trade agreement. On 1 January 1994, the North American Free Trade Agreement went into effect, and it included a provision for spirits. The three countries agreed to recognize Canadian Whisky, Bourbon Whiskey, Tennessee Whiskey, and Tequila as distinctive spirits of each home county. This gave tequila legal protections in its largest markets, and the CRT could focus its efforts on enforcement and promotion.

RIGHT Forteleza tequila is sold in hand-blown glass bottles.

ABOVE Copper stills in Jalisco.

The creation of the 1994 NOM and two minor updates helped propel tequila into its current position as the US's second most popular spirit by sales. By splitting tequila and 100% agave tequila into two separately labeled categories, brands such as Herradura, Patrón, and others were able to differentiate their products from "mixtos" (tequila made with a mix of sugars) and lean into stories of tradition and craftsmanship. Before the 100% agave category was created, these products were selling one-third of what mixto tequilas were. Within four years of the new classification, total sales had grown by more than 240% and, for the first time since 1964, 100% agave tequila sold more than mixtos.

However, from 2000 to 2006 there was drop in total sales of tequila and, once again, 100% agave fell into second place. The reason for this was not war or economic depression but nature itself. Beginning in the late 1980s, a pathogen swept through agave farms causing the leaves of weak plants to dry out and the hearts to putrefy in the field. This exposed the vulnerability of the tequila industry, which had come to rely on replanting clones of clones and decreasing genetic variation of the agaves in the fields. When pests and pathogens come to fields with a wide range of genetic diversity, some plants will die but many will survive. In a field full of clones, however, if one plant is susceptible to a disease, all of them are. The disease outbreak was followed in 1997 by an especially cold winter, which blanketed the highlands of Jalisco in snow for the first time in a century. Combined, the two unfortunate events wiped out a huge number of plants and created another shortage of blue agave.

The effects of this shortage had passed by 2005, when a flood of 100% agave tequilas began entering the market. This influx of products meant that new and old brands needed new ways to differentiate themselves for the ever-growing base of new tequila drinkers. Some brands focused on making "traditional" tequilas, with agaves cooked in brick ovens and crushed with volcanic stone, and the liquid fermented in wood tanks and distilled in small copper pots. Others, meanwhile, produced tequila that had been organically grown, was certified kosher, or labeled as gluten-free. (The US government has determined that all distilled spirits—by the nature of how they are made—are gluten-free, even if the spirit is distilled from grains. However, this has not prevented some brands from emphasizing that since agaves contain no gluten, their tequilas are gluten-free.)

The Great Additive Debate

With so many brands now on the market, people look for cues to indicate where and how they should focus their attention. For some, celebrity brands have been a huge draw into the world of tequila. Others want to support tequila brands that are Mexican, woman-owned, or both. There is another group that prizes authenticity in a brand, which, for many, means tequilas made without additives. Since August 2022 additive-free has quickly become one of the fastest growing search terms for tequila.

In 2013, Grover and Scarlet Sanschagrin saw an opportunity in the market and founded Tequila Matchmaker (now called Agave Matchmaker), an app and website that crowdsources tequila reviews from the public. As tequila fans themselves, the husband-and-wife duo used the platform to promote the spirit they loved and, with user-generated data, they tried to answer some common tequila questions. Queries such as: "Can you taste the difference between tequilas distilled in the highlands versus the Tequila valley?" Or, "Can you taste the difference between tequilas made with a tahona, versus a roller mill versus a diffuser?" One of the questions that kept coming up from users and journalists was, "What tequila brands were made without using any additives?" At the time, there was little transparency from tequila brands and no singular source of information so the Sanschagrins began collecting this information directly from brands. They found that there was a desire from some distilleries to better tell this part of their story.

In 2020, the Sanschagrin created the first additive-free certification for tequila brands—and they quickly met enthusiasm and resistance. This certification allowed a select number of brands and consumers to find each other. Consumers could have some confidence that a tequila's additive-free claim was true. However, the CRT was not happy with this development. Its position is that it is the only body legally authorized by the Mexican government to certify that any given tequila meets the requirement of the NOM, including the limits of allowed additives. In March 2023, the CRT announced that it was creating ITS own additive-free certification and that Patrón, the world's third largest tequila brand (as of 2024) would be the first to participate. But just ten months later, the CRT scrapped the program and stated that it had determined that no brand could claim to be additive free.

The fight over additive-free tequilas continued: in March 2024, Mexican authorities raided the Sanschagrins' home in Guadalajara while they were in New York. The authorities were acting on a report from the CRT that the Sanschagrin home was being used as "an adulterated tequila factory." The Sanschagrins decided to pivot and transform their Additive Free Alliance into a registered non-profit in the US and continue as an organization of "like-minded member companies that are committed to transparency, community, and honesty". However, by October 2024 the Sanschagrins allegedly got word that participating brands were having their export licenses threatened if they continued their participation. In response, the couple removed all tequilas from their online list of certified additive-free spirits. In the light of this, it is uncertain how the controversy over additive-free tequila will play out, yet the interest and excitement for tequila is continuing to grow.

The history of tequila shows us that life is a combination of both good times and bad, joys and sorrows. The Mexican people took the cataclysm of the Spanish Conquest and created an amazing spirit that the world now gets to enjoy. The noble agave is also a wonderful example of how struggle and persistence in life can bear great results. So, with more than 2,000 brands and 6,000 individual expressions, now is the time to dive into the world of tequila. Find a bottle or two that speaks to you and share it with others as we move through this life together.

TEQUILA TIMELINE

1530 The village of Tequila founded in Nueva Galicia

1569 Arrival of Filipino-style stills

1621 First written reference of a distilled vino de mezcal

1795 José María Guadalupe de Cuervo y Montaño receives first license to make vino de mezcal in Tequila

1953 Recipe for the Margarita published in Esquire

1964 Law updated so tequila can only be made from blue agave and no more than 30% of other sugars

1968 Boundaries of tequila restricted to Jalisco and areas of neighboring states

1970 Tequila allowed to be made with up to 49% other sugars

1971 Frozen Margarita machine invented

1972 Rolling Stones take the Tequila Sunrise on tour

1974 Mexico creates first denomination of origin for tequila

1976 DO expanded to include parts of Tamaulipas

1994 Updated law (NOM) defines Tequila, 100% Agave Tequila, and allows use of mellowing agents (abocantes)

Consejo Regulador Del Tequila founded to enforce the DO and NOM for tequila

NAFTA protects tequila as a unique Mexican spirit in the United States and Canada

1812 — Taberna de Cuervo renamed La Rojeña

1854 — First use of "tequila" to describe vino de mezcal made in the town of Tequila

1850s — First mezcal de Tequila sold in the United States

1870 — Herradura is founded in Amatitán, Jalisco, although it is not named Herradura until 1928

1873 — Cenobio Sauza founds La Perseverancia distillery in Tequila, Jalisco

1893 — Mezcal de Tequila earns gold at the Chicago World's Fair

1930 — First confirmed use of cane sugars in production of tequila

1930s — Invention of the Margarita cocktail

1949 — First law setting quality standards for tequila

2005 — NOM updated to include Extra Añejo Tequila

2005 — Sales of 100% Agave Tequila permanently overtakes mixto tequila

2010s — Many large brands transition to diffuser-made tequila

2020 — First list of "additive-free" tequilas created

2023 — Tequila overtakes American Whiskey to become the second most popular spirit in the United States

TIMELINE OF TEQUILA LAWS

Law	Production Area	Allowed Agave	Unique Production Requirements
DGN R-9-1949	Areas of Jalisco characteristic of agave cultivation.	100% agave: blue or others grown in the region	Distilled with fibers
DGN R-9-1964	All of Jalisco	Blue agave with up to 30% other non-agave sugars	Distillation with fibers no longer required
DGN R-9-1968	Jalisco and areas of neighboring states that are ecologically similar	No change	Required Lab Certification t verify batches were within specifications
DGN-V-7-1970	No change	Blue agave with up to 49% other non-agave sugars	No change
NOM DGN-V-7-1976	Jalisco and select municipalities in Nayarit, Guanajuato, Michoacán, and Tamaulipas	No change	No change
1974	Jalisco and select municipalities in Nayarit, Guanajuato, and Michoacán	No change	Tequila is a unique product of Mexico.
NOM-006-SCFI-1994	No change	No change	Allowable abocantes define to include caramel color, oa extract, glycerin, and sugar syrups. NOM number required on the label
NOM-006-SCFI-2005	No change	No change	No change
NOM-006-SCFI-2012	No change	No change	No change

Classifications	ABV Range	Post-distillation additions
Natural: Unaged Añejo: Minimum of 2 years in oak barrel.	45-50%	Natural: Only water Añejo: Sugar up to 5.4g/l
Blanco: Unaged Añejo: Minimum of 1 year in oak barrel.	38-55%	Blanco: Only water Añejo: Caramel coloring; sugar up to 1.0g/l
Blanco or Joven: Unaged Reposado: Rested in an oak barrel or on oak chips. No minimum time. Añejo: Minimum of 1 year in oak barrel.	No change	Blanco: Only water Reposado: Caramel coloring; no added sugar other than from wood or color. Añejo: Caramel coloring; sugar up to 0.7g/l
Blanco: Unaged; Joven removed Reposado: Minimum 2 months in an oak barrel Añejo: Minimum of 1 year in oak barrel; maximum of 600 liters	No change	None specified. Limits being studied by office of standards.
Blanco: Unaged must rest for minimum of 20 days Reposado: Minimum 4 months in an oak barrel Tequila defined as less than 100% agave 100% Agave Tequila created as separate class	No change	Maximum dry extract: Blanco 0.2g/l Reposado 0.5g/lAñejo 3.5g/l
No change	No change	No change
Tequila Categories: Tequila: Defined as less than 100% agave. 100% Agave Tequila. **Tequila Classes:** Blanco: Unaged; minimum rest time removed. Joven or Gold: Blanco with added mellowing or a blend of blanco and reposado. Reposado: Minimum 2 months in an oak barrel. Añejo: Same as 1976	35-55% ABV	Maximum dry extract: Blanco 0.2g/l Joven 5.0g/l Reposado 5.0g/l Añejo 5.0g/l
Extra Añejo: Minimum of 3 years in oak barrel; maximum of 600 liters	No change	No change
Blanco: Unaged or aged in oak for less than 2 months	No change	No change

2

If you look up the definition for tequila in a dictionary, you will learn that it is a type of liquor made from the agave plant in Mexico. While this definition is accurate, there is so much more that goes into the process of making tequila. It is the details—from how the plant is grown and cooked, and the juices extracted from its fibers, to how those juices are fermented and distilled—that make all the difference. Understanding these processes will help inform why certain tequilas taste the way they do, and why the simple combination of agave, yeast, and water can produce so many different expressions of tequila for the world to enjoy.

How Tequila is Made

The Agave Plant

Native to Mexico, agaves are part of the same family as asparagus, yucca, and lily of the valley. The agave's natural range extends from Northern California down to at least Peru. From there, agaves have spread around the world via either animals or people to locations including the Caribbean, Sicily, South Africa, India, and Australia. Agaves are their own genus that shares common characteristics such as: they are all succulents with leaves that grow in rosettes, and for the most part are all monocarpic, which means they only flower once before they die.

Within this genus, there are more than 250 recognized species of agave and hundreds of additional varieties and cultivars. However, only a fraction of these are regularly used to make spirits, with *Agave tequilana* being the most well-known. Until the 1970s, there were at least four varieties of *A. tequilana* commonly used to make tequila. Agave farmers and distillers referred to these by their common names: azul (blue), pata de mula (mule's foot), sigüín, and zopilote (vulture).

Rules for Tequila

In Mexico, there is an official registry that lists the legal standards for everything from units of measurement, to standards on specific types of pottery and for making tequila. This registry is known as the Mexican Official Standards, or Norma Oficial Mexicana (NOM). For tequila, the standards are listed in NOM-006-SCFI-2012 which govern the ingredients that are allowed in tequila, the strength at which it can be bottled, and defines several different categories and classes of tequila that can be sold. In general, tequila is a spirit distilled from a fermented mixture at least 51% sugars from the blue agave plant and no more than 49% sugars from other sources. Once distilled, the spirit can be bottled unaged or aged in oak containers. Before bottling, producers are also allowed to add both mellowing agents and other additives within certain limits, as well as demineralized water to reduce the strength of the tequila to between 35% and 55% alcohol by volume (ABV). These ingredients dictate whether the spirit can be labeled as tequila, 100% agave tequila, or flavored tequila.

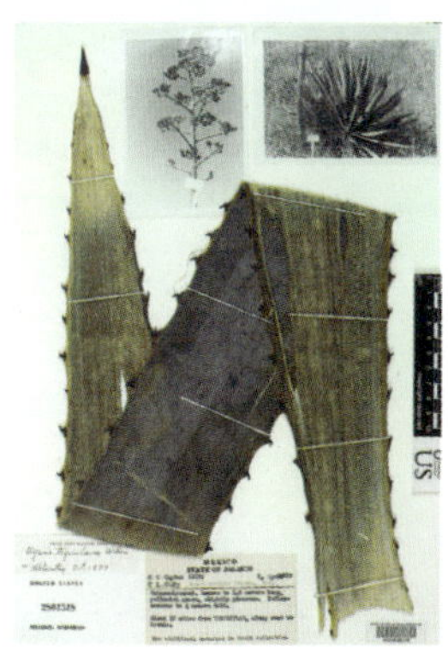

ABOVE A sample of *Agave tequilana F.A.C. Weber var. azul* from a scientific collection.

▼ Growing and Harvesting Blue Agave

Tequila can only be made from the blue agave or, more specifically, the *Agave tequilana F.A.C. Weber var. azul,* which gives the spirit its defining characteristics. Agaves are so different from any other plants used to make alcohol, that it is difficult to fully convey the uniqueness of these spirits without providing some detail about the biology and life cycle of these special succulents. Most crops used to make alcohol, such as barley, grapes, sugar cane, corn, apples, and even potatoes,

Life and Death of the Blue Agave

Over the millennia, blue agaves developed adaptations that allowed them to thrive in the semiarid landscape of western North America. One of these adaptations was to follow a nocturnal cycle. When the air is dry and the sun is beating down, the agave closes the pores on its leaves (stomata) that breath in carbon dioxide and exhale oxygen. This limits how much water each plant loses to evaporation. Then at night, when the relative humidity is often higher, the stomata open, the plant breathes, and new growth takes place. Because of its harsh environment, the blue agave developed two forms of asexual reproduction and one method of sexual reproduction to pass on its genetic information. With the first method, the agaves produce offshoots called hijuelos (E-wh-ell-lo-s) around the base of the plant that are exact genetic clones of the mother plant. Once the mother plant dies, the hijuelos continue to grow. Second, near the end of an agave's life it shoots up a large stalk, also known as the quiote (key-oat-tay) which can grow 16–20ft (5–6m) tall. As the quiote grows, it develops several bulbils along the stalk that are also clones of the mother plant. The bulbils act as a backup should the agave fail to produce seeds. This sometimes happens when animals or insects make a meal out of the quiote before its flowers are pollinated. Once the main plant dies and the quiote falls to the ground, some of these bulbils have the chance to survive and begin life again. The agave's final method to pass on its genes is to mate with another agave. At the very top of the quiote, dozens of flowers bloom. But, unlike other plants that close their flowers at night, nocturnal agaves have adapted to keep their flowers open day and night so that bats as well as insects and hummingbirds can collect the pollen while simultaneously fertilizing the seeds with their neighbor's pollen. Once fertilized, the seeds contain the genetic information of both plants. As the plant dies, the flowers transform into seedpods that, once dry, burst open and spread the seed on the ground. There they wait for the rains to come and the cycle begins again.

grow and are ready to harvest in one season. But it is common for agaves to take anywhere from five to 30 years before they reach maturity and are ready for harvest. This long growth period contributes to the complexity of the spirit, adds value, and makes the spirit special.

Farmers and distillers like working with the blue agave because of how easily it reproduces, its relatively short life cycle, and its high level of potential sugars. Almost all blue agave grown for tequila begin life as one of several cloned offshoots that grow directly from the mother plant. These agave offshoots are known as a hijuelos (E-wh-ell-lo-s), which translates as "pups." When they are three to six years old, each blue agave will sprout between three and seven hijuelos every year making it relatively easy to replace all the agaves harvested for tequila. Farmers will leave the hijuelos attached to the mother plant for a year before they carefully detach and transplant them into a new field.

As the blue agave grows, about 50% of its biomass forms in the leaves and the other 50% accumulates in the heart of the plant. The blue agave gets its name from the blueish-gray coloring of its leaves, known as pencas (Pen-Ka-s), which reach 5–7ft (1.5–2m) long as it grows. After five to eight years of growth, the heart of the plant weighs 66–308lb (30–140kg) and is full of water and a soluble fiber called inulin, which can be converted into fermentable sugars. Blue agaves, however, do not make it easy to access the inulin that it spent years accumulating as its energy reserves. Each penca has spines running up and down both sides and the tip has a long spine that can pierce through clothing and skin. In addition, once workers cut the pencas they secrete a sap made of saponins that can cause a rash when it comes into contact with bare skin.

To make just one liter of tequila, distillers need between 15 and 22lbs (7 and 10kg) of harvested blue agave. This physically demanding job goes to specialized workers called jimadors (He-Ma-Doors). Jimadors use a long pole with a rounded razor-sharp blade at the end called a coa de jima to slice through the pencas. Once a jimador has roughly cleared away the pencas they attack the base of the agave with their coa and

BELOW Cutting agave plants in Tequila, Jalisco.

Population Collapse and Bat-Friendly Agave

One serious downside to only replanting hijuelos is that it results in field after field of exact genetic copies. With so little genetic diversity, the whole population of blue agaves become vulnerable to future pests and diseases that could cripple the entire industry. If agave farmers allowed as few as 5% of their blue agaves to flower and produce seeds, botanist and ecologists believe this would create enough genetic diversity to prevent a population collapse. This would have the added benefit of providing a vitally important food source for the endangered Mexican long-nosed bat. Unfortunately, the present market does not offer agave farmers any economic incentive to leave 5% of their fields unharvested so reliance on hijuelos continues.

use the pole as a lever to detach the heart of the plant from the roots. After toppling the plant, the jimador then gives the agave a closer shave. At this point, the heart of the agave looks like a giant pineapple (piña) with a mostly white body and a blue green diamond lattice. Once shaved, workers load the piñas onto a truck headed to the distillery.

▼ Hydrolysis

Once the piñas arrive, the distillery must first convert the agaves' inulin into fermentable sugars. By applying heat in the presence of water, inulin's chemical bonds fracture to create smaller molecules of fructose and sucrose that yeast will consume to produce alcohol. This chemical process is known as hydrolysis. Generally, there are three different tools distillers use individually

RIGHT Cooked piñas ready to be removed from the autoclave.

ABOVE Hornos that are used to steam piñas.

or together to complete this process. These include brick ovens, known as hornos (hor-no-s), autoclaves, and diffusers.

Hornos are usually large brick rooms built side by side and with heavy doors to allow workers to load the piñas into the ovens. Distillery workers chop the piñas in half and then cut out the root of the quiote, which is called the cogollo (Ko-go-yo), because it is waxy and adds bitterness to the spirit. Once halved, the piñas are stacked inside the horno and are steamed for between 36 and 72 hours. At the beginning of the cooking process, the piñas sweat off a liquid called miel amarga (Me-el Ah-Mar-ga) or bitter honey, which is a combination of dirt, wax, and residual sap still in the plant. This bitter liquid falls into rows of narrow troughs that run the length of the floor, separating it from the cooking piñas. Hornos are less efficient than diffusers and autoclaves because, during the long cooking process, some of the inulin seeps out of the piñas before it is converted into fructose, which reduces the total yield of each batch. However, the longer cooking time also helps to develop more complex flavors in the final spirit.

Autoclaves cook the piñas in a similar fashion. However, the long, pressurized steel tubes cook more agaves in less time. They are essentially large industrial pressure cookers. Just as with hornos, distillery workers cut the piñas in half, remove the cogollo, and pack them inside the oven. A steel grate floor in the autoclave creates a small void where the miel amarga collects during the cooking process. Depending on how much pressure the autoclave uses, it can cook a batch of piñas in just 7 to 12 hours. Distilleries that use high pressure (above 1.5 atmospheres) will have a shorter cook time and those that use low pressure (between 1 and 1.5 atmospheres) will have a longer cook time. A shorter cooking time results in more of the piñas' inulin converting to fructose. This makes autoclaves more efficient in both time and total alcohol yield, while still creating some of the same aromas and flavors that develop with horno cooked agaves.

The final and newest tool created to convert the agave's inulin into fermentable sugars is the diffuser. The diffuser is a large machine that is 95 to 99% efficient at extracting inulin from raw agave and converting it into fermentable sugars without ever cooking the piñas. The process begins by loading raw piñas into the machine, which shreds or chips them into small pieces. The diffuser sprays the shreds with hot water to dissolve the inulin from the fibers. Depending on the distillery, there are a few different techniques used either individually or in concert to break the inulin into fermentable sugars. One method is to mix the inulin slurry with hydrochloric or sulfuric acid to chemically convert the inulin into sugar. Another is to pump the slurry into a large vertical autoclave that applies pressure and heat to break the inulin's molecular bonds. Some distilleries use a combination of the two. Diffusers are so efficient that they need as little as 5½lb (2.5kg) of agave to produce one liter of tequila, compared to the 15–22lb (7–10kg) with traditional cooking.

▼ Extraction

Once the piñas are cooked, they turn a deep caramel-like brown—this indicates that they are full of sweet agave juices that are ready to be extracted. In general, there are three methods for extracting juices from the agave fibers: a diffuser, a 2-ton (1.8 tonne) mill stone called a tahona (Tah-Ho-na), or a mechanical mill. Distillers have been using tahonas to make tequila for more than 300 years. These giant wheels are often carved out of volcanic rock, set in a circular pit, and attached by an axle to a center post. In the past, a team of mules would have pulled the tahona around the circle while workers loaded the trough with cooked agave. Tahonas are not the most efficient method to extract juices and they can take as long as a day and a half to process a batch of cooked agaves. By the 1960s, most tequila distilleries had abandoned the tahona for mechanical mills, which saved them both time and money. However a couple of brands, including Siete Leguas (*see* p. 160), continued the practice. Fast forward 40 years to the 2000s, and such brands claimed the tahona was key to the quality of their tequilas. Since then, a few dozen more distilleries have taken to using this age-old method to crush their agaves. Many of these brands have become cult favorites.

BELOW The cooked piña, with pulp.

ABOVE The Casa Siete Leguas, El Centenario distillery still uses traditional donkey-pulled tahonas to crush agave fibers.

Part of the inefficiency of tahonas is that although the wheel effectively pushes out the juices as it rolls over the agaves, the fibers reabsorb some of those juices once the weight is lifted. Because of this push and pull with the fibers, agaves crushed by tahonas can retain as much as 30% more of its juices. To mitigate this potential loss, some distillers will either ferment the extracted juices along with some of the fibers, or they will run the crushed fibers though a mechanical mill, squeezing out every last drop.

Most distilleries that use mechanical mills to extract the juices prefer roller mills, followed by screw mills in a distant second. With roller mills, distillery workers feed the cooked piñas through a shredder which makes it easier for the fibers to pass through the mills. A conveyer belt carries the fibers at an angle up to the first set of rollers. Before they reach the rollers, the mill sprays the fibers with water to aid extraction. The fibers then drop from the conveyer belt onto the mill, which contains two grooved cylinders that pull the fibers through a very narrow gap. The rollers squeeze out some of the juices which are diverted to a collection tank, while the fibers are placed on a second conveyer belt to repeat the process. Most roller mills have four or five mills that get progressively tighter so there is no juice left in the fibers by the end of the process.

The screw mill achieves the same result, though its mechanics differ slightly. As with roller mills, the process starts

RIGHT Roller mills at a distillery.

with distillery workers shredding the cooked agaves. Workers load the fibers into a hopper which feeds a metal corkscrew that carries the agave fibers through a narrow cylinder. The cylinder is covered by a fine metal screen; as the screw turns it squeezes the fibers against each other and pushes the juice out of the screen. Like roller mills, screw mills are very efficient at extracting the agave juices from the fibers but only a handful of distilleries use them.

Fermentation

After extraction, pumps fill large tanks with the agave juices and yeast to begin the fermentation process. It is also at this stage when the distillery decides if it is going to make a mixto or 100% agave tequila. If it chooses to make a mixto, workers fill the fermenter with a combination of agave juice and another sugar source, such as cane sugar or high fructose corn syrup. While the law allows up to 49% of other sugars by weight, some brands use much less. El Tequileño (*see* p. 113), for instance, makes its mixto with 70% agave and 30% cane sugar. There are even some mixtos on the market made from 99% agave with only 1% other sugars.

Once the fermenter is full the process of fermentation is largely the same whether it's for a mixto or 100% agave tequila. There are some minor differences such as the material the tank is made from (wood, cement, or stainless steel) or whether the tank has an open or closed top. These differences result in tequilas with different flavor profiles, but it is difficult to say with certainty that wood tanks produce x flavors while stainless steel tanks produce y flavors. One major difference that is noticeable in fermentation, however, is the type of yeast a brand uses. It is common to find that tequilas from the same distillery and produced in similar ways have similar profiles.

These types of shared characteristic usually come from the yeast, and it is part of what creates a house style from one distillery to another.

Yeast is a single-cell microorganism that has lived in symbiosis with humans for thousands of years. In tequila production, workers can either add one or more specific strains of yeast to the fermenters, or they can allow ambient yeast floating in the air to inoculate the tank. When yeast consumes sugar, it produces alcohol, CO_2, and small quantities of hundreds of other chemical compounds that create flavor. Many tequila distillers use yeasts that are especially adapted

to fermenting agave sugars, though some like to use other strains such as champagne yeast. In some rare circumstances, distillers will rely entirely on the wild yeasts in the air to ferment the contents of their tank. The use of wild yeast is ubiquitous in the world of mezcal but it is rare in the tequila world. This is because wild yeasts can take longer to ferment, they may not fully convert all the available sugars, and there is the possibility for them to produce flavors that the distiller or brand does not like.

Depending on the type of yeast used and the temperature, fermentation can take anywhere from 24 hours to 12 days. Some industrial strains of yeast are designed to work very quickly while maximizing alcohol production. However, this usually comes at the expense of flavor. Slower-working yeast may not be as efficient at producing alcohol but it can develop more complex flavors. Yeast doesn't like to be too hot or too cold. If yeast gets too hot, it gets stressed and starts to produce

BELOW The fermenter in action at Tapatio's La Alteña distillery.

off flavors and chemical compounds that result in a harsh spirit. If yeast gets too cold, however, its metabolism slows down and the fermentation process can stall leaving lots of unfermented sugars. During the summer months, distillers work to keep the yeast from getting too hot and stressed by using larger fermentation tanks that have more thermal mass and take more heat to warm up. Distillers can also use water on the outside of the tanks to help cool them down. In the winter, tequila distillers need to make sure the temperature doesn't get too low which would stop the fermentation process of the must (fermenting agave juice). Some tanks are fitted with stainless steel tubing that can circulate warm water to keep the yeast happy and producing the alcohols and flavors the distillers are looking for. At the end of this process, the must has a strength of between 4 and 7% alcohol by volume (ABV) and is ready to be distilled.

▼ Distillation

Distillation is the process of separating two or more components in a liquid based on their different boiling points. The reason we use distilling to make tequila, mezcal, or any other spirit, is because alcohol (specifically ethanol) boils at 78°C (173°F) and water boils at 100°C (212°F). The earliest evidence for distilling dates back almost 5,000 years to a clay still made around 3500 BC in what is today modern-day Iraq. However,

BELOW Stainless steel and copper pot stills at Tapatio's La Alteña distillery.

The Problem with Vinazas

Vinazas are often sprayed on fields as both a fertilizer and irrigation, but in high concentrations they are toxic. Vinazas are very acidic and have a very high oxygen demand so, if too much is dumped at once and it drains off into waterways, it can kill wildlife in the water and pollute the environment. Vinazas do this by lowering the pH of the water, which causes algae blooms that absorb much of the oxygen in the water, suffocating fish and other wildlife. Vinazas can be treated to make them less toxic to the environment but the current methods only begin to make economic sense at a large industrial scale. Historically, vinazas were used to create adobe bricks by combining them with clay, sand, and agave fibers. 818 Tequila (*see* pp. 68–69) has partnered with a non-profit called S.A.C.R.E.D to revive this practice and donate its adobe bricks to build a library, mezcal tasting room, and a community center in rural Mexico.

distilling technology didn't arrive in Mexico until the 1500s. But, by the early 1600s two different still types (Spanish and Filipino) had both been adapted to making agave spirits.

As with rum, whiskey and other spirits, tequila is made with both pot stills and continuous column stills. The pot still is a large vessel made from either copper or stainless steel and is usually heated with steam. As the fermented must is heated, vapors begin to rise from the liquid. As the vapors rise, they travel up through the neck of the still and over to a condenser where the vapors return to their liquid state. This first distillation results in a clear liquid called ordinario (Or-din-are-ee-o) that is between 20 to 25% ABV. Once the distiller collects enough ordinario it is redistilled a second time to make tequila. During the second distillation, the liquid is split into three phases. The first vapors that come over are called cabezas (Ka-bay-za-s) or heads, and consist of higher alcohols such as methanol and acetone. These are collected separately and discarded. The second phase is called the corazón (Kor-ah-zone) or hearts; these contain alcohol and water, as well as the esters and congeners that give tequila its unique flavor. The last phase is called the colas or tails, which is heavier and oilier. A small number of colas can help add texture and body to the spirit but too much can make the spirit hot and harsh on the tongue.

Column stills work on the same principle of separating liquids based on their boiling point but they are more efficient and everything is accomplished in one continuous process rather than in separate batches like the pot still. Fermented must is pumped to the top and then gravity pulls the liquid down the column while large amounts of steam are pumped in from the bottom. As the must and the steam meet, the heat causes the alcohol and other volatile compounds to boil and rise toward the top of the still. As these vapors rise, they recondense on perforated plates inside the still and re-vaporize as they are hit with more steam. This process of vaporizing, condensing, and re-vaporizing repeats again and again throughout the entire height of the still, causing alcohol vapors to concentrate near the top while most of the water and all the solids fall to the bottom. This spent liquid, also known as vinazas (VIN-ah-sah-s), is pumped out of the still and collected. Once distillation is complete, the collected corazón is tequila that can be bottled immediately as a blanco tequila or transferred to oak barrels to age.

▼ Maturation

As with whiskey and rum, tequila was originally stored in barrels so that it could be shipped from one place to another but, eventually, people began to enjoy the flavor of these tequilas. Because of the high temperatures, high elevation, and dry air in central Jalisco, tequilas barrels can lose as much as 10% of their volume to the angel's share (evaporation) per year. The NOM for tequila specifies that it can be aged in either "roble" or "encino" (two common names for different species of oak) containers. In practice, most tequila is aged in used 53 gallon (200 liter) American whiskey barrels. French oak and used wine barrels are common though less widely used.

Aging tequila in oak barrels has two primary effects, the extraction of color and oak flavors from the wood and a mellowing of the spirit through oxidation. As the temperature of the spirit rises and falls over the course of days, months, and years, it is pushed in and out of the wood absorbing both water and alcohol soluble compounds such as vanillin, caramelized wood sugars, and tannins. Oxygen is also the driver of a complex set of chemical reactions that break down certain compounds and form new ones helping the spirit to evolve and develop more complex flavors. But, because of the relatively short aging period for tequilas (less than 12 months for reposado and less than 3 years for añejo), there is a limit to how much color and flavor the spirit can develop—especially if the barrel has been filled multiple times. The best distilleries use this to their advantage by using multiple types of barrels (ex-wine, ex-whiskey, French oak, American oak, Hungarian oak etc.) as well as barrels that have been refilled multiple times, or re-charred to increase the available wood flavors, sugars, and color. However, it requires more complex record keeping and skill to manage and blend from all these barrels while maintaining consistent flavor profiles for all their various expressions. This is why some distilleries and brands have

ABOVE Tequila aging in barrels at the Jose Cuervo Fábrica La Rojeña distillery.

decided instead to use mellowing agents (abocantes) to more precisely control the color, flavor, and mouthfeel of their tequila.

Additives and Abocantes

In certain circumstances, the NOM for tequila allows distillers to use additives and abocantes in their spirit. According to the NOM, additives are a long list of ingredients that include sweeteners, colorants, and flavorings meant to substantially intensify the color, aroma, and/or flavor of the tequila and which must be listed on the label. Tequilas with additives are just flavored tequilas, such as coconut-, jalapeño- or hot pink grapefruit-flavored tequila. You know these have additives because the brand will list the added flavor or color somewhere on the front or back label.

Abocantes on the other hand do not need to be labeled if they stay under a certain threshold. Generally, when the average person refers to additives, they are really thinking of abocantes which the NOM defines as caramel coloring, natural oak extract, glycerin, and/or sugar-based syrups. Because tequila will absorb different amounts of color from each individual barrel, caramel coloring can be used to standardize the color of the spirit from batch to batch and bottle to bottle. The tequila industry is not alone in this practice; the use of caramel coloring is also allowed in Scotch whisky, rum, and cognac production. Oak barrels, if properly maintained, can remain water tight for decades but they can become exhausted of their flavor and color after just a few uses. In these circumstances, oak extract can provide added oak flavor and tannins to the spirit which may not have been available in older barrels. Glycerin is a sugar alcohol derived from either plants or animal fats and is used in many foods and cosmetics. In tequila, glycerin can add body to the spirit, giving a fuller and smoother mouthfeel as well as a light sweetness. And, lastly, sugar syrups can add both sweetness and body to a spirit, and make rough-tasing spirits more palatable. This too is common practice in the world of spirits. Rum, cognac, and Canadian whiskies can all be sweetened to enhance their flavors.

The NOM says that only gold, reposado, añejo, and extra añejo tequilas can include abocantes. It also says they can have no more than 1% abocantes by weight but the wording is a little vague as to whether that means 1% in total or up to 1% for each of the four abocantes allowed. Later in the NOM, it specifies that these tequilas can have no more than 5g/liter of dry extract which would include added abocantes as well as wood tannins and color naturally absorbed by the spirit during maturation. In practice, when the Tequila Regulatory Council (CRT) tests batches of tequila to see if they comply with this rule, it is measuring whether the spirit comes in at or below the dry extract threshold of 5g/liter.

BELOW Caramel coloring is one of the most commonly used abocantes.

The real controversy around abocantes is not that they are allowed, but the perceived lack of transparency around their use, and the belief that some brands use them as a back door to artificially flavor tequilas without having to label them as such. For a subset of consumers, the use of "additives" has become a contested issue. Their argument is not that they are inherently bad, but they believe that brands are being dishonest for using abocantes to significantly manipulate a tequila's flavor while portraying an image of traditional production that only includes the use of blue agave, yeast, oak, and water. It is natural to expect that tequila aged in ex-bourbon barrels for a year or more will likely pick up light flavors of vanilla and caramel. However, if a reposado tequila tastes strongly of vanilla and birthday cake, there is no conceivable way that the intensity of that flavor was achieved just through the interaction of spirit and oak. There are lots of people who will enjoy drinking that tequila and there is nothing wrong with that. But some consumers are left with a bad taste in their mouth because their expectation of how the NOM regulates the use and labeling of abocantes and additives does not match what they taste out in the market.

ABOVE Bottling at Don Cayo.

Proofing and Bottling

Before a distillery bottles its tequila, it needs to reduce the spirit with water to its desired strength. Depending on the distillery, the tequila will come off the still or out of the barrel between 55 to 75% ABV, but Mexico does not allow them to bottle tequila above 55% ABV. In practice, the bottling strength for each brand and expression will change depending on where the bottles are intended to be sold. In Mexico, the minimum bottling strength is 35%, in the UK it's 38% ABV, and in the US it is 40% ABV. While most tequilas sold in those countries are at or close to the minimum bottling strength, there is a current trend for high proof or still strength tequilas that are bottled between 50 to 55% ABV. A small handful of brands have always had at least one high strength expression, but the number of them has been growing since 2023. When a batch of tequila is ready to be bottled, distillers add it to a proofing tank and only then can water be added to dilute the spirit to bottling strength. Once proofed, the spirit is allowed to rest briefly to allow the water and alcohol to integrate before it is pumped to the bottling line to be filled and packaged.

TEQUILA PRODUCTION

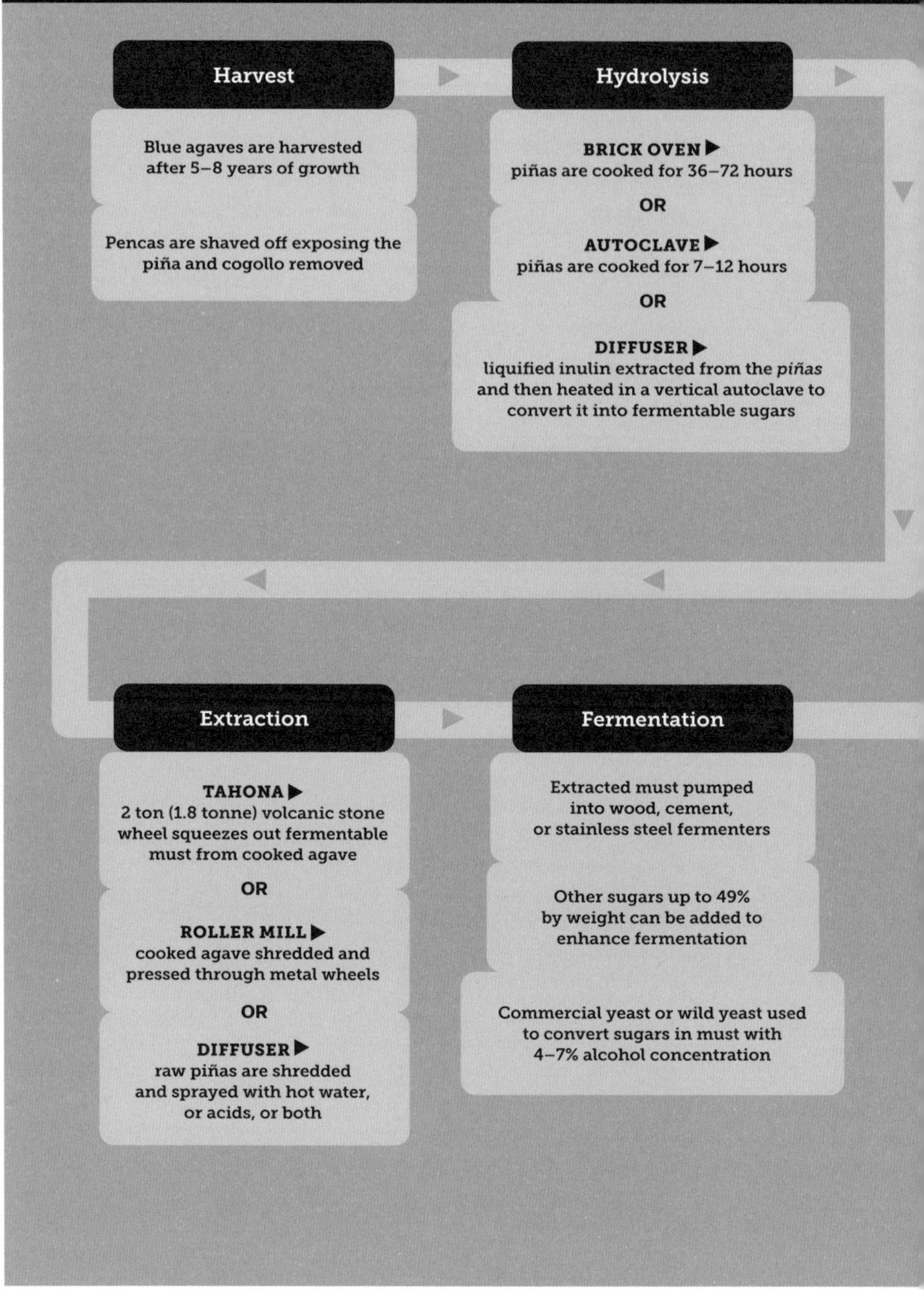

Harvest

Blue agaves are harvested after 5–8 years of growth

Pencas are shaved off exposing the piña and cogollo removed

Hydrolysis

BRICK OVEN ▶
piñas are cooked for 36–72 hours

OR

AUTOCLAVE ▶
piñas are cooked for 7–12 hours

OR

DIFFUSER ▶
liquified inulin extracted from the *piñas* and then heated in a vertical autoclave to convert it into fermentable sugars

Extraction

TAHONA ▶
2 ton (1.8 tonne) volcanic stone wheel squeezes out fermentable must from cooked agave

OR

ROLLER MILL ▶
cooked agave shredded and pressed through metal wheels

OR

DIFFUSER ▶
raw piñas are shredded and sprayed with hot water, or acids, or both

Fermentation

Extracted must pumped into wood, cement, or stainless steel fermenters

Other sugars up to 49% by weight can be added to enhance fermentation

Commercial yeast or wild yeast used to convert sugars in must with 4–7% alcohol concentration

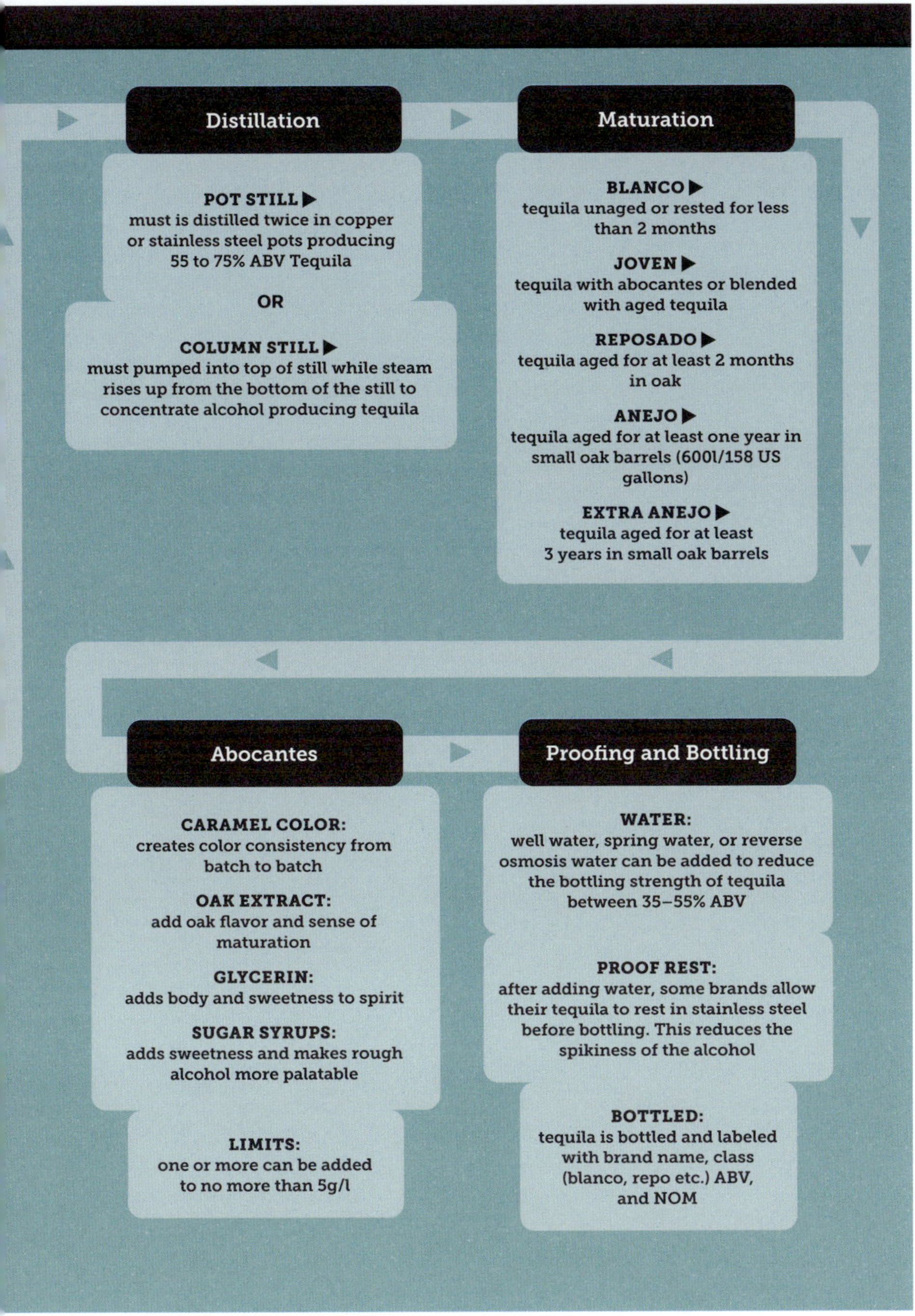

Distillation

POT STILL ▶
must is distilled twice in copper or stainless steel pots producing 55 to 75% ABV Tequila

OR

COLUMN STILL ▶
must pumped into top of still while steam rises up from the bottom of the still to concentrate alcohol producing tequila

Maturation

BLANCO ▶
tequila unaged or rested for less than 2 months

JOVEN ▶
tequila with abocantes or blended with aged tequila

REPOSADO ▶
tequila aged for at least 2 months in oak

ANEJO ▶
tequila aged for at least one year in small oak barrels (600l/158 US gallons)

EXTRA ANEJO ▶
tequila aged for at least 3 years in small oak barrels

Abocantes

CARAMEL COLOR:
creates color consistency from batch to batch

OAK EXTRACT:
add oak flavor and sense of maturation

GLYCERIN:
adds body and sweetness to spirit

SUGAR SYRUPS:
adds sweetness and makes rough alcohol more palatable

LIMITS:
one or more can be added to no more than 5g/l

Proofing and Bottling

WATER:
well water, spring water, or reverse osmosis water can be added to reduce the bottling strength of tequila between 35–55% ABV

PROOF REST:
after adding water, some brands allow their tequila to rest in stainless steel before bottling. This reduces the spikiness of the alcohol

BOTTLED:
tequila is bottled and labeled with brand name, class (blanco, repo etc.) ABV, and NOM

3

When you pick up a bottle of tequila, the label will tell you quite a bit of information about the liquid contained inside—especially if you know what to look for. Mexico requires labels to list certain pieces of information while others are added by brands as part of their marketing strategy and for points of differentiation. It is also true that a label may not tell you everything you want to know, and in some cases may be slightly misleading. This is why it is important to know how to read a tequila label and understand what is—and isn't—being said. The following guide will define some of the most common tequila terms found on labels.

How to Read a Tequila Label

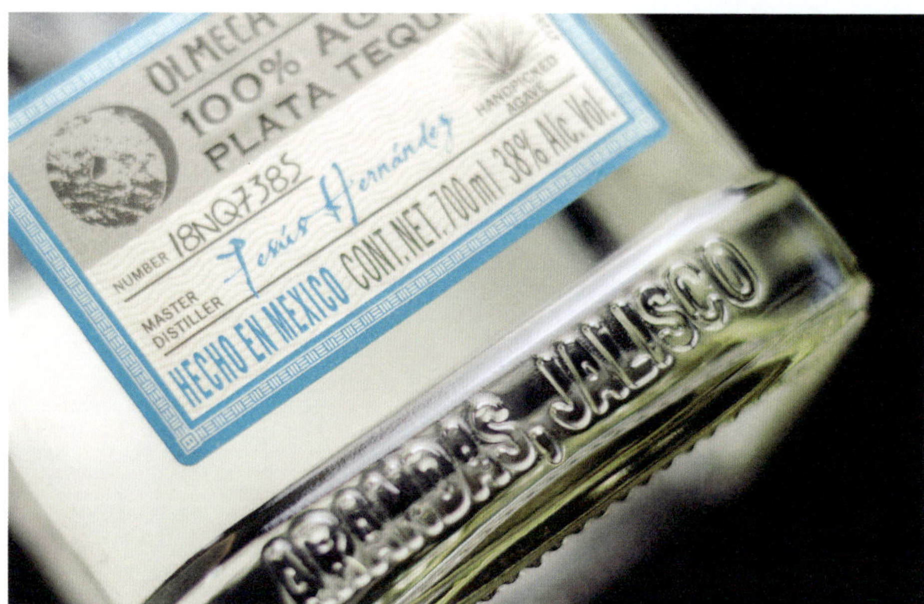

Brand Name

The brand name is often the most prominent text on the label and is the primary name by which brands identify themselves. In the world of tequila, it is common for third parties to own brands that are separate from the distillery and importer. The CRT keeps an updated list on its website of all certified brands, along with the company name, address, and NOM numbers of the authorized producer that bottles the brand.

Authorized Producer

A company certified by the CRT to produce tequila in accordance with NOM and that is physically located within the boundaries of the denomination of origin (DO) for tequila. The name or address of the authorized producer can be listed either on the front or back label and is not always the common name for the distillery. For example, the authorized producer, Tequila Tapatio, owns the distillery La Alteña where it produces the brand El Tesoro for Suntory Global Spirits, but on its US labels the producer is identified as La Alteña. Because of the variations in how this information is listed on different labels, it is usually best to identify the producer by the NOM number on every bottle of tequila.

NOM Number

This is the four-digit number found on every bottle of tequila. For example, "NOM 1234." This number is listed on either the front or back label and is usually listed next to or directly underneath the initials NOM. Every authorized producer has a unique NOM, though if a producer owns multiple locations the NOM can refer to any one of them.

CRT

Consejo Regulador Del Tequila (Tequila Regulatory Council) is a private non-profit that, at present, is the only organization accredited by the Mexican government to regulate the production of tequila and to enforce the current NOM for tequila. The CRT is funded by the Mexican government as well as a fee paid by brands and authorized producers to certify their products and facilities.

D.O.P.

Denominación de Origen Protegida (Protected Denomination of Origin) or D.O.P. is a type of geographical indication (GI) that Mexico uses to protect the names of unique food products from specific geographic regions. World Trade Organization members have agreed to recognize GIs and offer some basic reciprocal protections against the use of the protected name for products made outside of its recognized region. In 1974, the Mexican government created the first D.O.P. to protect tequila. Before this, Mexico had passed laws internally to define where and how tequila could be made, but other countries did not recognize those laws. Today, tequila's DO declares that tequila is a unique product of Mexico that can only be produced in 181 specific municipalities across the Mexican states of Jalisco, Michoacán, Guanajuato, Nayarit, and Tamaulipas.

ABV

Alcohol by volume is a measure of the strength or concentration of ethanol in a liquid. According to the Mexican government, tequila can be bottled between 35 and 55% ABV, however, the lower limit can be restricted by the laws of the country the tequila is exported to. The minimum strength for tequila in the UK is 38% ABV and in the US is 40% ABV. And, though both the UK and US allow spirits sold above 55% ABV, there are no tequilas sold abroad that are above the Mexican limit.

Tequila

A regulated term for a regional spirit distilled from the ferment of no less than 51% blue agave sugars and no more than 49% other sugars by weight and bottled between 35 and 55% ABV. Informally, this type of tequila is referred to as mixto, because it is made by co-fermenting a mix of agave and other sugars. Mixto tequilas cannot be made by blending blue agave spirit and spirits made from other sources such as cane spirit. Once distilled, tequila can be bottled unaged, aged in oak barrels, and/or mellowed with the addition of caramel coloring, oak extract, glycerin, and/or sugar syrups up to 5g/liter by dry weight (also known as abocantes). The use of abocantes does not need to be labeled, but if other sweeteners, coloring agents, aromatizers, and flavorings are added, they must appear on the label.

100% Agave Tequila

A regulated term for a regional spirit distilled from the ferment of 100% blue agave sugars and bottled between 35 and 55% ABV. This can appear on the label as 100% agave, 100% de agave, 100% puro de agave, or 100% puro agave. Like mixto tequilas, 100% agave tequilas can be bottled unaged, aged in oak barrels, mellowed with abocantes (unlabeled), or include additives if they are labeled. For many years, 100% agave was a marker of quality that could distinguish traditionally made tequilas from mixtos. However, since the introduction of the diffuser which extracts agave sugars without cooking the piñas, the 100% agave label on its own is not as strong an indication of quality as it once was.

Blanco

Also labeled as white, silver, or plata, blanco is a regulated labelling term for mixto and 100% agave tequilas that are either unaged or rested in oak for less than two months. Blancos must be transparent though not necessarily colorless, and they can only be diluted to bottling strength with water. Officially, abocantes are not allowed in blanco tequila, but the NOM does allow up to 0.3g/liter of dry extract. Presumably, this is to account for any solids derived from any brief aging in an oak barrel, but the NOM does not seem to prevent distillers from adding flavorings to a barrel and then dumping them out before it is filled with tequila.

Gold Tequila

Also referred to as Joven (young) or Oro, gold tequila is a regulated labelling term for mixto and 100% agave tequilas. Though in practice, most gold tequilas are mixtos that get their golden hue from the addition of caramel coloring and smoothed out with the addition of glycerin or sugar syrup. Officially, gold tequilas can be made either by blending blanco tequila with abocantes, or by blending a blanco tequila and an aged tequila (reposado, añejo, or extra añejo). Gold tequilas are allowed to have up to 5 g/liter of dry extract from the addition of abocantes or aged tequila. Generally, gold tequilas are value products that are mostly used for mixing with soda or in cocktails.

Reposado

A regulated labelling term for mixto and 100% agave tequilas that have been aged in an oak container for a minimum of two months and less than 12 months. Reposado translates into English as rested, though the NOM only allows reposado to be labeled as "Aged" if the Spanish term is not used. Reposados can be blended with older tequilas; if the youngest spirit in the mixture is less than 12 months it must be labeled as a reposado. Reposados can also contain abocantes up to 5g/liter of dry extract.

Añejo

A regulated labelling term for mixto and 100% agave tequilas that have been aged in an oak container, no more than 600l/158 US gallons in volume, for a minimum of 12 months and less than three years. Añejo translates into English as "old," though the NOM only allows añejos to be labeled as "extra-aged" if the Spanish term is not used. Añejos can be blended with older tequilas, but if the youngest tequila in the mixture is less than three years old, it must be labeled as an añejo. Añejo tequilas may contain abocantes up to 5g/liter of dry extract.

Extra Añejo

A regulated labeling term for mixto and 100% agave tequilas that have been aged in an oak container, no more than 600l/158 US gallonsin volume, for a minimum of three years. While it is possible to have a mixto as an extra añejo, in practice only 100% agave tequilas are sold as extra añejos. The term Extra Añejo was added to the NOM in 2005 because there was a growing number of brands selling tequilas that were aged much longer than the one-year minimum threshold for añejo. The term Extra Añejo translates into English as "extra old," although the NOM only allows extra añejos to be labeled as "Ultra-aged" if the Spanish term is not used. Extra añejo tequilas may also contain abocantes up to 5g/liter of dry extract. In the tequila world, extra añejos are unofficially abbreviated as XAs.

Cristalino

An unregulated term that refers to barrel-aged tequilas (reposados, añejos, or extra añejos) that have had the color stripped out to make the spirit crystal clear. The first cristalino tequila came to the market in 2008, though the practice of filtering color out of aged spirits had been common practice in the rum world for decades. Cristalinos were developed for customers who want to drink tequilas that have the flavor and maturity of an aged spirit but without any of the color. Some people prefer clear spirits for esthetic reasons, and some bartenders like to use decolorized spirits to preserve the color of a cocktail without adding color from the spirit. Cristalinos are made by filtering aged tequila through pulverized or powdered activated carbon. Once crushed, activated carbon has a large surface area with thousands of micropores that absorb color compounds. The goal is to produce a crystal-clear tequila with all the same aromas and flavors as an aged tequila, though this is not always easy to achieve.

Rosa

An unregulated term that refers to tequilas that have a rose color hue from resting or aging in freshly emptied red wine barrels. According to the Real family (*see* p. 77), they began making a rosa tequila back in the 1950s though this new category did not emerge into the consumer consciousness until the release of the celebrity owned Calirosa in 2021. Since then, a growing number of brands have released their own rosa tequilas, which are bottled either as blancos (rested for less than two months), or reposados.

OPTIONAL MARKETING TERMS

Tahona

Sometimes referred to as an Egyptian mill, a tahona is a very heavy stone or concrete wheel set in a shallow pit to crush cooked agaves. Before the advent of mechanical shredders or diffusers, the tahona was an advancement in tequila production that replaced hand-milling agave. Around the 1960s, tequila distillers began to phase out their mule or horse drawn tahonas in favor of mechanical mills. Today, there are a little over a dozen distilleries that use tahonas to make tequila and, except for Siete Leguas (*see* p. 160), all modern tahonas are motorized.

Estate

This is an unregulated term that can refer either to where the agave was harvested or where the tequila was bottled. The idea of estate-grown agave was borrowed from the wine world and implies that the brand gets all its blue agave from fields that it controls versus purchasing agave from independent farmers. While neither is inherently better, estate-grown agave can give the impression that the brand has more quality control over the entire tequila-making process. Other brands promote that their tequilas are estate-bottled, which doesn't seem to mean anything more than the spirit was bottled at the distillery where the tequila was made.

Kosher

A mark that indicates a tequila's production and bottling process has been inspected by one of several kosher certifying agencies and independently certified that it was made in accordance with the Jewish dietary laws. Because tequila is made from blue agave, it is not too difficult for a brand to qualify as kosher. It is possible for a tequila to be disqualified from receiving a kosher certification if the producer uses non-kosher commercial yeast, or if the spirit was mellowed with the addition of glycerin, as it can be derived from animal fats. This means that many mixto tequilas would not qualify as kosher.

Organic

A mark that tequila brands can acquire from one of a few different organizations that certifies their tequila is made with organic ingredients. In the context of tequila, this means that the blue agave was grown organically (without the use of synthetic fertilizers or pesticides) and fermented with wild yeast and/or an organic commercial yeast strain. If abocantes or additives were used in the tequila, they would have to be derived from organic sources as well. Organic foods have become a massive market driven primarily by consumers who are concerned with the quality of the ingredients in their food and drinks.

Premium

This is an unregulated marketing term used to indicate a particular tequila is of superior quality and to justify a higher price point. Brands use terms including premium, super-premium, and ultra-premium, to imply the quality of their ingredients, the craftsmanship that went into making the product, and its rarity. These terms are shorthand descriptions for a suggested retail price band for a spirit. Premium tequilas are those priced slightly above the cheapest value brands, super-premium tequilas indicate a higher-than-average price, and ultra-premium tequilas are a more exclusive and costly tier above that.

High Proof / Still Strength

An unregulated term that refers to tequilas that are bottled at or above 50% ABV. There has always been a handful of tequilas bottled at higher ABVs, but for much of tequila's history it has been bottled at or near its minimum, partly because there is less tax on lower ABV spirits. A trend in high proof or still strength tequilas began in 2023.

Lot/Batch number

In 1994 the NOM defined a lot as batch of tequila produced within the same time period. Every lot must be labelled and tracked so the CRT can perform its required tests that ensure each batch complies with the regulations for the tequila's class and category. Once bottled, the producer must engrave or mark each bottle with the lot number from which it was filled. This way if there happens to be any contamination or a test batch does not meet the standards for tequila, the CRT can track down the other bottles from that same lot and pull them from the market. In addition to these regulatory purposes, some collectors use the lot numbers as a way to track subtle changes in their favorite tequila's profile over time.

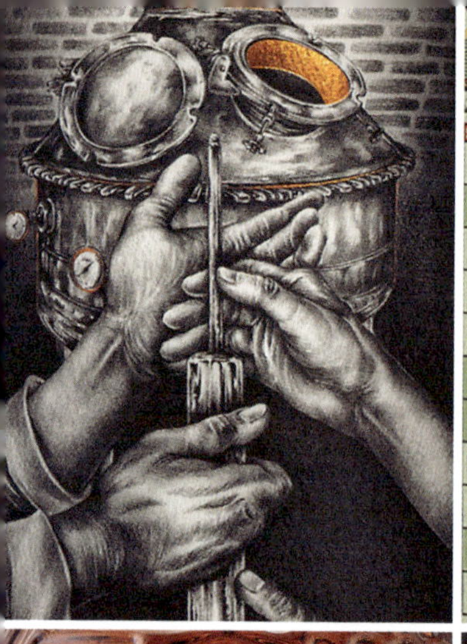

TEQUILA
LA JUVENTUD

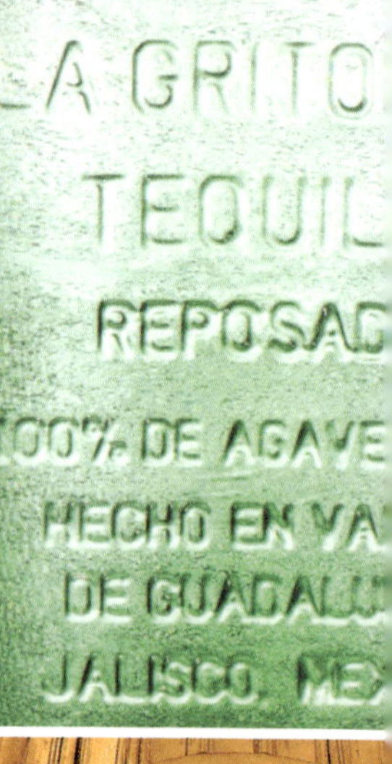
LA GRITO
TEQUIL
REPOSAD
100% DE AGAVE
HECHO EN VA
DE GUADAL
JALISCO, ME

PASOTE
TEQUILA

HECHO EN TAMAULIPAS
UN TEQUILA EXCEPC
1972
G.G.D.L.
Chinac
AÑEJO
40% ALC. BY VOL. | NET. CONT.
100% PURO AGAVE

TEQUILA
OCHO

QUILA
100% Aga
Viejit
PLATA
50% Alc. Vol. (100 Proof)
Net. Cont. 750 ml

TEQUILA
TROMBA
REPOSADO
LOS ALTOS
HECHO EN MEXICO
JALISCO
100% de Agave

blanco
100% DE AGAVE
suerte
TEQUILA

THE TEQUILAS

Over the last decade, the tequila world has exploded, and there are well over 6,000 different expressions available for purchase. There is no way to include so many tequilas in a compact book such as this, so I endeavored to taste a representative sample at a variety of price points. After sampling close to 250 expressions, these are my comprehensive tasting notes. The tequilas are organized alphabetically by brand name to make them simple to find. The tasting notes are designed to help you, the reader, discover the tequila flavors you prefer and, in turn, which expressions appeal to your palate.

The Tequila Profiles

AGE RANGES:

Blanco: Unaged or aged less than 2 months.
Reposado: Aged a minimum of 2 months but less than 12.
Añejo: Aged a minimum of 12 months but less than 3.
Extra Añejo: Aged a minimum of 3 years.

CATEGORIES:

Mixto Tequila: Made from 51 to 99% blue agave.
100% Agave Tequila: Made from only 100% blue agave.

PRICE RANGES

$ = <$35
$$ = $35-$59
$$$ = $60-$99
$$$$ = $100-$199
$$$$$ = $200+

Price Ranges are approximate US retail prices at the time of publication. These will vary by location due to local taxes. Ranges are intended as a general sense of where the tequila falls in the spectrum from value tequilas to prestige brands.

RANKINGS:

No ranking, stars, or points are given to the tequilas because these give the illusion of objectivity, when everyone's palate is different. People will prefer some tequilas over others for a variety of personal reasons that cannot be validated by simple score.

Drinking Recommendation Key

There is no correct or incorrect vessel from which to drink tequila. Jicaras, veladoras, tumblers, champagne flutes or even Riedel's specially designed tequila glasses can all enhance the drinking experience at the right place and time. However, if you want to practice noticing the aromas and flavors in your tequila, a standard Glencairn glass will do the job nicely. They are very sturdy, relatively inexpensive, and easy to purchase. The shape helps to concentrate the aromas of the tequila just above the rim of the glass where your nose is. Tequila has a higher ABV than wine, so it is not necessary to stick your nose in the glass.

Key
The key below indicates what kind of drinks work well with each tequila on the following pages

Drink neat

Serve direct from the freezer

Drink with water

Serve in a cocktail

 Serve on the rocks

Serve with soda (soda water or sweetened soda)

Casa Cuervo first released 1800 Tequila in 1975 as a reposado-only brand. Initially called Cuervo 1800, it was a premium tequila bottled in a decanter with a glass stopper. Over time, Cuervo slowly expanded the brand to include Reserva Antigua 1800 Añejo Tequila in 1997, a blanco in 2004, the Milenio in 2014, and a cristalino in 2020. 1800 is bottled in a unique trapezoid-shaped bottle, that's designed to resemble a Mayan pyramid—which also helps it stand out from all the other round bottles. According to Cuervo, 1800 was released in honor of the first year that the La Rojeña distillery aged tequila in oak barrels. Cuervo initially released Milenio as a onetime limited-edition tequila to celebrate the beginning of the new millennium. However, in 2014, the growth in the ultra-premium tequila market encouraged it to re-release it to compete with the likes of Don Julio 1942 (*see* p. 107) and Avión Reserva 44 (*see* p. 75). Milenio was designed as a "tequila for whisky drinker[s]" and uses some of Cuervo's oldest tequilas.

1800

NOM
1612

Region
Central

Distillery
1800 Distillery

Category
100% Blue Agave Tequila

Hydrolysis
Horno

Extraction
Roller Mill

Still Type
Copper Pot Still

Brand Owner
Casa Cuervo

Blanco

Strength
40% ABV

Price
$$

FLAVOR This tequila offers cooked agave, plum, and pepper aromas, with a sweet-sour taste. The finish is long, semidry, and fruity, evolving from plum to watermelon bubble gum. It's a lightly fruity option recommended for mixing or drinking on the rocks.

Reposado

Strength
40% ABV

Price
$

FLAVOR A reposado with light aromas of cooked agave, black pepper, oak, and vanilla, which intensify over time. The flavor starts sour and bitter, evolving into sweet vanilla, lemon, green agave, and lime zest, with oak building to a sweet, woody profile. The finish is long and dry with oak and lemon notes; it's a decent but rather unremarkable reposado best enjoyed on the rocks or mixed.

Añejo

Strength
40% ABV

Price
$$

FLAVOR With aromas of red grapes, plums, nectarines, oak, and leather, this tequila has a palate that is fruity with notes of red grapes, stone fruits, oak, vanilla, and baking spices, with cinnamon and cloves intensifying on the second sip. The finish is long and semidry, with lingering flavors of clove, cinnamon, oak, leather, and dried dates, making it a pleasant, oak-forward añejo suitable for neat sipping, on the rocks, or in the Distrito Federal (*see* p. 194).

Cristalino Añejo

Strength
40% ABV

Price
$$$

FLAVOR This cristalino has a light ethanol aroma with lime zest and hints of wet stone. Initially, it tastes sweet, then becomes dry and sharp, with peach, banana, and cooked agave flavors. The finish is semisweet with notes of peaches, plums, vanilla, and oak, making it a good option for fruity cocktails or sipping chilled from the freezer.

Milenio Extra Añejo

Strength
40% ABV

Price
$$$$$

FLAVOR This tequila has a light woody aroma with notes of oak, baking spices, vanilla, and hints of agave and black plums. On the palate, it is warm, sweet, and full of wood spices, ripe plum, light caramel, and full-bodied oak, with an underlying sweetness from cooked agave and panela (unrefined cane sugar). Milenio is a very lovely oak forward extra añejo (XA) that celebrates the warm spices and woody sweetness that can come from long aged tequila.

Hector Galindo Miranda and three friends launched 4 (Cuatro) Copas Tequila in 1997, named after one of their favorite songs, Cuatro Copas by José Alfredo Jiménez. In the 2000s, Hector transitioned ownership to the De Anda Orozco family of Arandas, Jalisco, which had been growing agave for four generations. According to the brand, it produced the first certified organic and kosher tequila, and it also makes one of the few tequilas fermented entirely with wild yeast. In 2020, its Añejo earned gold at the American Distilling Institute's International Spirits Competition and was named Best Tequila and Best International Agave Spirit of the Year. Two years later, the brand permanently included a 110 Proof bottling. Until 2023 when it moved from NOM 1480 to NOM 1522, 4 Copas' tequilas were distilled by Sebastian Melendrez, the former master distiller for Herradura (*see* p. 128). It is now distilled by Iliana Partida, a fourth-generation master distiller from the famed Partida family.

4 Copas

NOM
1522

Region
Los Valles

Distillery
Hacienda de Oro, Amatitán, Jalisco

Category
100% Blue Agave Tequila

Hydrolysis
Horno

Extraction
Roller Mill

Still Type
Copper Pot Still

Brand Owner
Verde Tequila

Blanco

Strength
40% ABV

Price
$$

FLAVOR There is a rich aroma of brown sugar and baked yams in this tequila, with lighter notes of wet stone and fruit. On the palate, it offers an explosion of sweet tropical fruits and cooked agave flavors, with a tart citrus finish. This is a really nice and well-made blanco that I'd suggest sipping neat or using in any of your favorite tequila cocktails.

Blanco 110

Strength
55% ABV

Price
$$$

FLAVOR This tequila has sweet fruit aromas of mango, banana, and lime, followed by a strong alcohol note. The palate is sweet yet dry, and it is bursting with ripe fruit flavors such as banana, strawberry, mango, lime, and apricot, evolving with cooked agave, dry grass, and pepper. Overall, a powerful and tasty blanco that pairs nicely with dry vermouth in a tequila martini with a twist of lemon.

Reposado

Strength
40% ABV

Price
$$$

FLAVOR This reposado's fantastic aroma has notes of guava, lemon-lime, tangerine, apple, and cooked agave. On the palate, it's juicy with flavors of cooked agave, oak, lime, and overripe pineapple, balanced by a slight grassy character. This is fun and fruity, blending nicely with a small amount of oak.

Reposado 110

Strength
55% ABV

Price
$$$

FLAVOR This tequila offers aromas of dried plums, cooked agave, and lemon blossoms, with a spicy, fruity, and grassy flavor. With each sip, the flavors intensify, showing more heat and dry oak tannins. It has a long, semisweet finish with lingering dried fruit and oak flavors, making it a bold and fruity reposado recommended for those who enjoy dried fruit notes with agave and oak.

Añejo

Strength
40% ABV

Price
$$$

FLAVOR This has a powerful aroma with notes of lime zest, orange blossom, and cooked agave. On the palate, it's silky smooth with oak, vanilla, lemon, black pepper, and green agave flavors. The finish is long and dry with a slight tingle and flavors of cut grass, lime zest, and vanilla. A lovely, flavorful tequila with finesse.

Añejo 110

Strength
55% ABV

Price
$$$$

FLAVOR An añejo with a powerful nose of white pepper, vanilla, and wasabi, evolving into plum and oak. The palate is dry, spicy, and sweet with flavors of oak, tobacco, pepper, red grapes, plums, cooked agave, and caramel. The extra alcohol makes it a little dryer, but the combination of flavors is fantastic.

818

This celebrity-owned tequila brand secretly entered several competitions—and won top awards—in 2020 before it began selling bottles the following year. In June 2021, 818 announced it was committing 1% of its revenue to fund a variety of environmental and community impact projects and later partnered with a non-profit called S.A.C.R.E.D. (Saving Agave for Culture, Recreation, Education, and Development) to oversee several projects in Mexico such as the construction of a library and middle school in Zapotitlán de Vadillo, Jalisco. The buildings were constructed from adobe bricks made in part from agave fibers and vinazas, the liquid left over from distilling tequila. A year later, 818 launched Eight Reserve, which comes in a custom ceramic bottle sourced from Pachuca, Mexico and it moved from NOM 1137 to partner with NOM 1607, which is more aligned with 818's environmental and community projects. The distillery itself runs partially on solar power and biofuel briquettes, made from the leftover agave fibers.

NOM
1607

Region
Los Valles

Distillery
Grupo Solave, Amatitán, Jalisco

Category
100% Blue Agave Tequila

Hydrolysis
Horno

Extraction
Tahona

Still Type
Copper Pot Still

Brand Owner
818 Spirits

Blanco

Strength
40% ABV

Price
$

FLAVOR This tequila has a unique fruity, funky, and earthy aroma, with notes of raspberry and cooked agave. On the palate, it offers fermented raspberry, baked yam, and white pepper. While it is a little rough when served neat, its surprising profile is a welcome addition to the flavor spectrum of tequila and worth trying.

Reposado

Strength
40% ABV

Price
$$

FLAVOR A tequila offering aromas of vanilla frosting, lemon zest, strawberries, cream, and black pepper. The palate balances sweet and acidic flavors, including vanilla, tart strawberries, lemon, Greek yogurt, and oak, and it has an odd tingling sensation. Overall, the flavors are pleasant if you enjoy sweet vanilla-forward reposados.

Añejo

Strength
40% ABV

Price
$$

FLAVOR This tequila has light aromas of sweet tarts, vanilla, and lemon zest. The palate features distinct raspberry, brown sugar, and cooked yam flavors, evolving to green apple, strawberry, and vanilla custard. The finish is semisweet and tart with lingering strawberry, whipped cream, and oak notes, making it a bright and fruity option for cocktails or ranch water (*see* p. 210).

Eight Reserve Añejo

Strength
40% ABV

Price
$$$$

FLAVOR Offering a light, wine-like aroma, this tequila has notes of plum, strawberry, vanilla, and earthy agave. On the palate, it's juicy with notes of lemon zest, oak, vanilla, baking spices, and cloudy apple juice. After swallowing, your mouth salivates from the high acidity and the flavor finishes with a combination of citrus, earth and cooked agave that will work nicely in an Old Fashioned (*see* p. 187).

ArteNOM is the brainchild of Jacob Lustig, who spent a couple of decades working with mezcal and tequila distillers. His idea was to create a brand that highlighted the best expressions from individual artisans and the impact of the terroir on tequila. This was initially blocked because CRT rules do not allow one brand to source from multiple distilleries but the CRT was petitioned and they made an exception. Lustig launched ArteNOM in 2010. ArteNOM Selección de 1123 is made by the Rosales family at Cascahuín (*see* p. 84) and highlights historical tequila production techniques that were common around 1900. After distillation, the tequila is mellowed in used mezcal barrels for 21 to 28 days and bottled at 43% ABV.

ArteNOM 1123

NOM
1123

Region
Los Valles

Distillery
Tequila Cascahuín, El Arenal, Jalisco

Category
100% Blue Agave Tequila

Hydrolysis
Horno

Extraction
Roller Mill

Still Type
Copper and Stainless Steel Pot Still

Brand Owner
Las Joyas del Agave

Blanco Histórico

Strength
43% ABV

Price
$$$

FLAVOR The aroma is deep and earthy with pleasant vegetal aromas of cut grass and white pepper. This is followed by a light fruity note, such as the skin of a Mexican cream guava or the juice from a ripe Meyer lemon. On the palate, there are flavors of cut grass and wet rock, followed by a light sweetness from cooked agave and a note of grilled pineapple. There is a slight warmth on the tongue like a mild chili that comes from the alcohol. ArteNOM Selección de 1123 is a classic lowland tequila with its deep earthiness. The contrasting vegetal and light fruit notes make this an enjoyable tequila to sip neat or with a couple dashes of water to open the spirit.

ArteNOM 1146

ArteNOM Selección de 1146 is a tequila that celebrates the artistry of Enrique Fonseca. This tequila is made using highland grown agaves from the fields surrounding Atotonilco el Alto, which are transported to Fonseca's distillery in the city of Tequila. After cooking, the extracted agave juices are fermented using a special strain of wine yeast and distilled to about 53% ABV before aging. This añejo is vatted from a selection of tequilas aged between 14 months and three years in French oak barrels, which previously held Cabernet Franc wine from the Loire Valley in France. This blend of tequilas is aged for an additional 12 to 14 months in a combination of Canadian whisky and Tennessee rye whiskey barrels. Finally, the finished tequila is proofed and bottled at 41.3% ABV.

Añejo

Strength
41.3% ABV

Price
$$$$

FLAVOR This tequila has a fantastic nose full of fruit flavors, such as ripe strawberry and rich blackberry jam. This is followed by notes of cinnamon, sandalwood, and cedar. Layered underneath these warm aromas are deeper scents of raisin, date, and dried plum. The aroma follows perfectly onto the palate with a symphony of spice and dried fruit flavors. On the tongue, the spirit is dry but there is a deep sensation of sweetness such as you might find in the best XO cognacs. The finish is long and dry with lingering flavors of oak, cooked agave, warm cinnamon, and dried apricots but without the acidity. This is a great tequila that deserves to be savored slowly and with intention. Put away your media because ArteNOM Selección de 1146 is this evening's entertainment. Sip neat and you may come to understand why Enrique Fonseca is known as the master of aged tequila.

NOM
1146

Region
Los Valles

Distillery
La Tequileña, Tequila, Jalisco

Category
100% Blue Agave Tequila

Hydrolysis
Low Pressure Autoclave

Extraction
Screw Mill

Still Type
Copper Pot Still

Brand Owner
Las Joyas del Agave

After the Mexican Revolution, the Vivanco family began cultivating agaves and, about 80 years later in 1994, it purchased Destilería El Ranchito. For Selección de 1414, the agaves are grown in the highlands surrounding Arandas and cooked in brick ovens for 36 hours. After the juice is extracted, it is pumped into stainless steel vats and left to ferment by the wild yeast floating in the distillery air. The must is double distilled to 56% ABV and matured for four months in third-fill bourbon barrels. After four months rest, the tequila is vatted and proofed to 41.2% ABV.

ArteNOM 1414

Reposado

Strength
41.2% ABV

Price
$$$

NOM
1414

Region
Los Altos Sur

Distillery
Destilería El Ranchito, Arandas, Jalisco

Category
100% Blue Agave Tequila

Hydrolysis
Horno

Extraction
Roller Mill

Still Type
Copper Pot Still

Brand Owner
Las Joyas del Agave

FLAVOR The tequila opens with a light and mineral aroma. On the palate, the flavor starts with vegetal notes of corn husk, green agave, and young oak. These are followed by sweet flavors of orange, sweet oak, a hint of vanilla, and some baking spice. There is a pronounced bourbon character to this reposado that blends well with the earthy and vegetal character of the underlying tequila. ArteNOM Selección de 1414 is a very green and vegetal reposado, so if you like that character in your blancos and are looking for something similar with a light barrel influence then this is the tequila for you. Despite their third use, the bourbon barrels add a layer of complexity and a light sweetness that the blanco likely doesn't have on its own. This tequila is best enjoyed neat, with a splash of water or as a highball with a twist of lemon.

ArteNOM 1579

Felipe Camarena makes Selección de 1579 and it is an example of a classic blanco tequila from the highlands. The agaves are grown around the town of Jesús María at 6,200ft (1,890m) above sea level and they are cooked for 30 hours in stone ovens. The agave fibers are crushed in a specially constructed metal wheel that acts in a similar way to a tahona. Rainwater is added to the juice and fibers to adjust the sugar levels to the ideal concentration for fermentation. The must is double distilled to 56% ABV, and proofed with a blend of rainwater and filtered well water down to 40.7% ABV.

Blanco

Strength
40.7% ABV

Price
$$$

FLAVOR This tequila has an intense aroma of cut grass that's sitting in the summer sun. It is bright, green, floral, and vegetal with a note that reminds me of dandelion sap. As it sits, the vegetal quality expands to include notes of orange leaves, tobacco, dried oak leaves, and the aroma of green acorns. On the palate, there are bright vegetal notes of green agave with a dash of warm cinnamon followed by flavors of fresh citrus, unripe papaya, and orange blossom mixed with a hit of white pepper heat. ArteNOM Selección de 1579 is a masterpiece that completely captures the flavors and aromas of highland tequila made by one of its great masters. While the intense vegetal character will not be to everyone's liking, it is perfectly balanced and has complete harmony between the aroma, flavor, and finish.

NOM
1579

Region
Los Altos Sur

Distillery
Destilería El Pandillo, Jesús María, Jalisco

Category
100% Blue Agave Tequila

Hydrolysis
Horno

Extraction
Tahona

Still Type
Copper Pot Still

Brand Owner
Las Joyas del Agave

Sommelier Richard Betts launched Astral Tequila in 2006. For much of the brand's life, Astral was sold only as a blanco made at NOM 1137. Betts wanted something that stood out so the original blanco was bottled at 46% ABV. Astral's production moved to NOM 1607 after being purchased by New York-based Davos Brands in 2017, and then global player Diageo in 2020. This shift produced a few changes: the tequila's strength was lowered to 40% ABV and Diageo also added a reposado and an añejo, the latter aged for 13 months in ex-bourbon barrels, to the lineup. Like 818 (*see* pp. 68–69), Diageo supports the production of adobe bricks by Grupo Solave and it has partnered with Habitat for Humanity Mexico. In the first year. it built ten new homes in Jalisco using adobe bricks. If you try Astral, the reposado is the best of the three core expressions.

Astral

NOM
1607

Region
Los Valles

Distillery
Grupo Solave, Amatitán, Jalisco

Category
100% Blue Agave Tequila

Hydrolysis
Horno

Extraction
Tahona

Still Type
Copper Pot Still

Brand Owner
Diageo

Reposado

Strength
40% ABV

Price
$

FLAVOR The aroma is light with a pronounced minerality along with softer notes of oak and vanilla. As the aroma builds, stronger notes of vanilla are followed by tart red berries. On the palate, the tequila starts sweet with flavors of vanilla and caramel and then it turns somewhat bitter with flavors of oak and lime peel. The finish is long and semisweet with a nice acidity that calls you back for another sip. Overall, this is a standard reposado that is mostly dominated by oak and vanilla. If you enjoy those flavors and want a tequila that isn't overly sweet, then you may enjoy this expression from Astral. This tequila is best enjoyed mixed with soda or used in cocktails that need a sweeter vanilla-forward tequila.

Avión

Avión was founded in 2009 by Ken Austin and Kenny Dichter, two former executives at a private jet rental company—which is where the brand gets its name. Avión launched with tequila made at NOM 1416 and, in 2013, it debuted Reserva 44 as its first extra añejo expression. When it came out, the tequila had been aged for a minimum of 44 months; however, that has dropped over time to 36 months. Today, Avión explains the name as referring to the 44 flavor notes found in the tequila. Avión did something right because it quickly gained the attention of drinks giant Pernod Ricard, which entered a joint venture with the brand to distribute the tequila around the world. In 2014, Pernod Ricard purchased a majority ownership stake in the brand for an estimated $100 million, and just four years later bought out the remaining stake.

NOM
1111

Region
Los Altos Sur

Distillery
Pernod Ricard Mexico, Arandas, Jalisco

Category
100% Blue Agave Tequila

Hydrolysis
Horno

Extraction
Roller Mill

Still Type
Stainless Steel Pot Still

Brand Owner
Pernod Ricard

Reposado

Strength
40% ABV

Price
$$

FLAVOR This tequila offers aromas of lemon and lime, toasted oak, and unripe pineapple, with a sweet floral and fruity taste that continues on the palate, featuring lychee, oak, vanilla, lemon, and cooked agave. The finish is medium-long and semisweet, with lingering white fruit and floral flavors supported by oak. If you are a fan of lighter-style tequilas with some oak influence, this is a great example.

Reserva 44 Extra Añejo

Strength
40% ABV

Price
$$$$

FLAVOR This offers strong vanilla, milk chocolate, and caramel aromas, with hints of agave and lime zest emerging later. On the palate, it's warm and sharp with vanilla, caramel, oak, and a spicy, rye-like character, balanced by an evolving agave presence. A sweet, wood-forward XA that has good balance and will be enjoyed best on the rocks or in cocktails.

Cabo Wabo

NOM
1440

Region
Los Altos Sur

Distillery
Destiladora San Nicolas, San Ignacio Cerro Gordo, Jalisco

Category
100% Blue Agave Tequila

Hydrolysis
Low Pressure Autoclave

Extraction
Roller Mill

Still Type
Column and Pot Still

Brand Owner
Campari Group

In 1996, Sammy Hagar, the former lead singer of the band Van Halen, became the sole owner of a restaurant and nightclub called Cabo Wabo in Cabo San Lucas, Mexico. Not long after, Hagar began sourcing tequila for the bar from Tequila el Viejito (*see* p. 117). By 1999, Hagar was sourcing his Cabo Wabo tequila from NOM 1426 and signed a deal with Wilson Daniels to import it into the US. The brand was immediately successful, and by 2006 it was the second bestselling tequila in the US after Jose Cuervo (*see* p. 132). In 2007, Hagar sold 80% of the tequila brand to Campari for $80 million and two years later Campari purchased the remaining shares for $11 million. After that, Campari moved Cabo Wabo to NOM 1440 where it is still made. The brand differentiates its tequila with the claim that it takes wider heart cuts, which includes more heads and tails than other brands to deliver "a more unfiltered" flavor. Cabo Wabo's aged tequilas are rested in American oak barrels—two months for its reposado, and 12 months for its añejo.

Blanco

Strength
40% ABV

Price
$$

FLAVOR This blanco has an aroma of vanilla and wet stone, evolving into butterscotch. It offers sweet caramel and butterscotch flavors, intensifying with each sip and reminiscent of Pusser's Rum. If you want a blanco that tastes like a sweet aged rum then this is the tequila for you.

Reposado

Strength
40% ABV

Price
$$

FLAVOR This reposado offers strong vanilla and lime zest aromas, evolving to include green agave, oregano, and oak. The palate begins sharp but mellows to sweet cooked agave, vanilla, and finishes with flavors of lemon and birchwood. This is a fun and zesty reposado that has a good balance between the agave and wood flavors, though the alcohol is a bit sharp to enjoy neat.

Celebrity couple Adam Levine of Maroon 5 and model Behati Prinsloo launched Calirosa in July 2022. The tequila comes out of NOM 1459, which has been owned by the Real family since 1942. According to the brand, the Real family created the rosa style tequila when it accidentally received red wine barrels to age its tequila instead of the whiskey barrels it had ordered. However, it seems that the first tequila exclusively aged in wine barrels came out of NOM 1500 back in 2017: Codigo 1530 Rosa Blanco. That said, Calirosa rests its blanco tequila in Californian red wine barrels for one month, which is enough time for the spirit to pick up a light rose color. In addition to the blanco, Calirosa distils a reposado, añejo, and a three-year and a five-year XA.

Calirosa

Blanco

Strength
40% ABV

Price
$$

FLAVOR The nose of this tequila is bright and fruity with notes of strawberry, orange zest, lime juice, and a touch of green agave. The palate starts semisweet with bright notes of pink lemonade, fresh strawberries, and lemon and lime zest. The finish is medium long and dry with notes of citrus peel, under ripe strawberries and it ends earthy. This is the perfect introductory tequila for the rosé wine drinker in your life. You can drink it on the rocks or with soda. It will also work in cocktails, but if you are using citrus juice or orange liqueur you might lose the tequila flavor in the mix.

NOM
1459

Region
Los Valles

Distillery
Tequila Selecto de Amatitán, Amatitán, Jalisco

Category
100% Blue Agave Tequila

Hydrolysis
Horno

Extraction
Roller Mill

Still Type
Copper Pot Still

Brand Owner
222 Spirits Company

While working as a tequila consultant in 2003, Sophie Decobecq began creating and tweaking her own tequila, collecting wild yeast samples to test which would produce the best flavors. Decobecq eventually found three yeast strains she liked best and established Calle (Kai-Yay) 23 in 2009 so that she could share her creation with the world.

Initially, Decobecq worked with NOM 1529 to produce her tequila, but she moved to NOM 1433 in 2015, and then to NOM 1545 several years later. This was in part because it allowed her to run the entire production process from start to finish. Unlike other brands that contract with a distillery to make a tequila for them, Decobecq rents out the distillery to produce her own spirit. The blanco and añejo are fermented with the first two yeast strains (A and B), while the reposado is fermented with the first and third yeast strains (A and C) as she felt that they were better suited for a lightly aged tequila.

Calle 23

NOM
1545

Region
Los Altos Sur

Distillery
Hacienda Capellania, San Jose de Gracia, Jalisco

Category
100% Blue Agave Tequila

Hydrolysis
Low Pressure Autoclave

Extraction
Roller Mill

Still Type
Stainless Steel Pot Still

Brand Owner
Tequila Calle 23

Blanco

Strength
40% ABV

Price
$$

FLAVOR The blanco has aromas of alcohol, lime zest, orange juice, and pineapple. It starts sweet on the palate but turns dry and bitter, with vegetal notes of white pepper and underripe plantains. This is a solid no nonsense tequila ideal for those who enjoy vegetal blancos. It may be a bit rough served neat but it will work in cocktails.

Reposado

Strength
40% ABV

Price
$$

FLAVOR This tequila has a soft mineral quality, with sweet aromas of cooked agave, caramel, and fruity notes such as pineapple, green apple, and red grapes. The palate features cooked agave, caramel, birchwood, lemon zest, pineapple, and a balance of earthy, floral flavors. This is a solid tequila that, while a touch hot served neat, is suitable for mixing or on the rocks.

Familia Camarena

In 1761, Mauricio and Juan Carlos Camarena co-founded the town of Arandas, Jalisco. Today, the Camarena family is a key family in the tequila world who, over the years, has married into the other historic tequila families of Mexico. One branch is now led by Mauricio Camarena, who takes his name from his 18th-century ancestor, as well as being a descendant of Don Eduardo Orendain, the founder of Arette Tequila on his father's side, and Don Jose Cuervo on his mother's side. Mauricio launched Familia Camarena Tequila in 2010.

The Familia Camarena tequila is made by fermenting the aguamiel (sweet agave juices) with a proprietary yeast strain developed for the Camarenas at the National Autonomous University of Mexico. By 2017, the brand was doing so well that it built a new distillery, NOM 1596, to solely produce the Familia Camarena Tequila. This was also the year that the family added an añejo tequila as a regular part of the brand's lineup

NOM
1596

Region
Los Altos Sur

Distillery
Casa Tequilera Herencia de Los Altos, Jesús María, Jalisco

Category
100% Blue Agave Tequila

Hydrolysis
Horno and Autoclave

Extraction
Roller Mill and Diffuser

Still Type
Column and Pot Still

Brand Owner
Familia Camarena

Reposado

Strength
40% ABV

Price
$

FLAVOR On the nose, this tequila has sweet notes of dried and candied pineapple which is layered with aromas of cooked agave. The first sip reveals flavors of sweet pineapple and a light dryness from the oak. With the second sip, you get more oak tannins but the overall flavor remains the same. The finish is semidry and medium-long. The sweet pineapple flavors persist on the tongue and, as they fade, a soft oak character reveals itself and then disappears. This reposado is almost identical to the silver tequila but with some added complexity from resting in oak. If I had to choose, the reposado offers a little more enjoyment when drinking for almost the same price—and it will work just as well in cocktails that call for blanco or reposado tequila.

Casa Dragones

NOM
1489

Region
Los Valles

Distillery
Destilería Leyros, Tequila, Jalisco

Category
100% Blue Agave Tequila

Hydrolysis
Acid-Thermal Hydrolysis

Extraction
Diffuser

Still Type
Column Still

Brand Owner
Casa Dragones Tequila Company

Maestra Tequilera Bertha González Nieves, a Mexican businesswoman, and Robert Pittman, creator of MTV, founded Casa Dragones in 2009 with the intention of creating a luxury spirit. At the time, Pittman owned a home in San Miguel de Allende, Guanajuato, called Casa Dragones, that served as the clubhouse and stables for the Dragones cavalry unit stationed there during the war for Mexican independence. González Nieves and Pittman launched the brand with their joven tequila, which is made from a blend of blanco and a small amount of "extra-aged" tequila. Extra-aged is the official English translation approved by the CRT for añejo tequilas, not extra añejos. As the tequila is crystal clear, it is fair to assume that it is charcoal-filtered to remove any color from the resulting blend of tequilas. Over time, Casa Dragones has also added a blanco, reposado, and an añejo to its portfolio. Casa Dragones says that it uses a modern and sustainable production process that allows it to use less agave per liter of tequila produced and less energy than other traditional methods. This most likely means that the brand uses a diffuser and acid-thermal hydrolysis which is more efficient at extracting and converting inulin into fermentable sugars. And, according to the brand, it proofs its tequilas using spring water that goes through a "state-of-the-art purification process"—which is probably a reverse osmosis water filter.

Blanco

Strength
40% ABV

Price
$$$

FLAVOR The aroma is light and fruity with notes of key lime, green agave, mineral water, and white pepper on watermelon. The palate is sharp and sweet with flavors of cooked yams, lemon zest, bubble gum, black pepper, cucumber, and tart berries. This is a high-acid tequila that will work well in highballs or a Ranch Water (*see* p. 210)—just skip the lime.

Joven

Strength
40% ABV

Price
$$$$$

FLAVOR This tequila offers aromas of moss, wet stones, green agave, and white pepper. It has soft flavors of green agave, cut grass, ginger, and lemon, with a medium-dry finish. The tequila is OK but given its price you may want to taste a pour before committing to a full bottle. Try it neat or over one large ice cube with a twist of lime. More than that will overpower it.

Reposado

Strength
40% ABV

Price
$$$$

FLAVOR This tequila has a light, floral aroma with notes of strawberry, white pepper, and earth. On the palate, it offers light flavors of cooked agave and orange blossom, followed by a tingling sensation and bright, spicy oak notes. Its unique character and price point make it hard to recommend for a typical drinker, though shaking it on ice enhances its sweet and floral notes.

Añejo

Strength
40% ABV

Price
$$$$

FLAVOR This tequila has a light, fruity nose with notes of bubble gum, strawberry, vanilla, and an inviting earthiness. On the palate, it's warm and slightly sharp with flavors of raspberry, lemon zest, and resinous oak. This is a unique and potentially polarizing tequila that may be enjoyed by those who like the warm resinous quality you sometimes get from a juniper-forward gin.

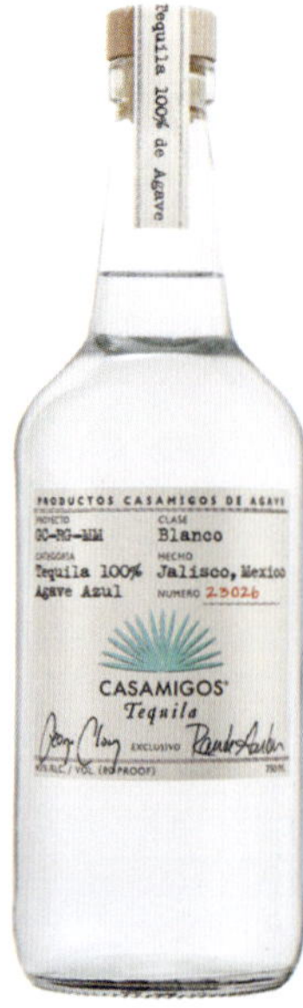

George Clooney, along with businessmen Rande Gerber and Mike Meldman, launched Casamigos tequila in 2013. According to Gerber, he and Clooney had both purchased property in Cabo San Lucas and each built a home on their property that they named casamigos (house of friends). And, since they both liked tequila, they decided they needed their own "house" tequila, so they began buying the spirit directly from NOM 1416. There is an apocryphal story that the reason they chose NOM 1416 was because it was the original home of Clase Azul (*see* p. 91) and Gerber, Clooney, and Meldman wanted a similar tequila. According to Gerber, after years of buying large quantities of tequila, the distillery said they needed a license—which put them on the road to formalizing the brand. Casamigos sold very well and was purchased by Diageo for $1 billion in 2017. For the next three years, NOM 1416 continued to produce tequila under contract until Diageo completed construction of NOM 1609 to produce all Casamigos tequila. Casamigos released its cristalino in 2023, which is made by filtering its reposado through charcoal to remove the color.

Casamigos

NOM
1609

Region
Ciénega

Distillery
Diageo México Operaciones, Atotonilco el Alto, Jalisco

Category
100% Blue Agave Tequila

Hydrolysis
Horno

Extraction
Roller Mill

Still Type
Stainless Steel Pot Still

Brand Owner
Diageo

Blanco

Strength
40% ABV

Price
$$

FLAVOR This tequila has a light, sweet aroma of melon and fresh orange juice that becomes dominated by notes of vanilla frosting and birthday cake. The palate starts with bitter citrus, then becomes sweet with vanilla and lemon zest. Vanilla frosting and birthday cake are not traditional blanco flavors but if you enjoy them, there's nothing wrong with that.

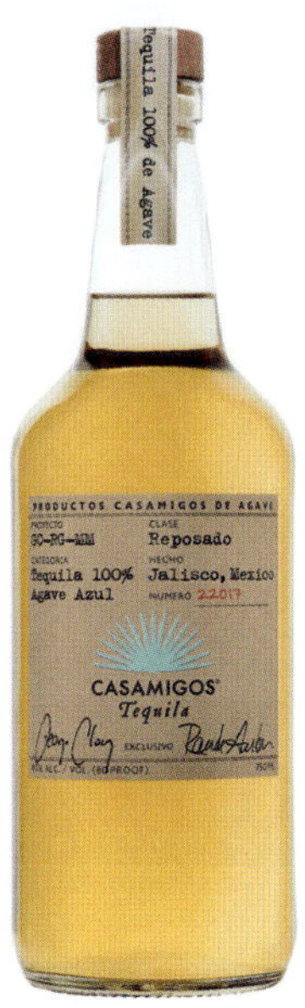

Reposado

Strength
40% ABV

Price
$$

FLAVOR This tequila offers strong aromas and flavors of milk chocolate, cocoa nibs, sea salt, vanilla, and caramel. The palate becomes bitter with notes of dark roasted coffee and raw wood. It tastes a bit like bitter gas station coffee with creamer. It's baffling how these intense flavors have been developed in a reposado. If you like dark chocolate and vanilla, try it in an Irish coffee with whipped cream.

Cristalino Reposado

Strength
40% ABV

Price
$$

FLAVOR This tequila has light aromas of mint, key lime, vanilla, and faint cooked agave that evolves into raspberry and blackberry. The palate is sharp, sweet, and dominated by vanilla and red berries, with a slight bitterness. If you try it, this reposado cristalino is best enjoyed with soda.

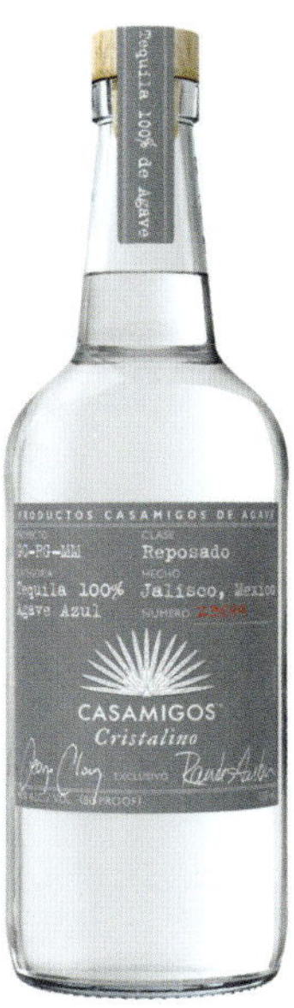

Añejo

Strength
40% ABV

Price
$$

FLAVOR This tequila offers aromas of wet stone, cooked agave, plum, caramel, oak, and vanilla that moves towards Jet-Puffed marshmallows. The palate is rich with vanilla and caramel, and is balanced by oak and a fleeting earthy agave note. The finish is semisweet with more vanilla and caramel that then turns to bitter grapefruit pith. If you enjoy vanilla-forward añejos, try it on the rocks or with cola.

The Rosales family founded Cascahuín in 1904, though the current distillery wasn't built until 1955. The name Cascahuín comes from a pre-Hispanic word that roughly translates as "hill of light" or "party on the hill." The tequila uses blue agaves grown in the valley surrounding El Arenal which are harvested at a lower Brix (potential sugar content), so it has become known for its intense herbaceous and vegetal flavor profile. This is common for spirits distilled from agaves with less sugar (think mezcal made from the *agave karwinskii* species); because the plants have less sugar per kilo of agave, the spirit has more green aromas and flavors. Cascahuín's process begins with agaves cooked for 30 hours in brick ovens. For its standard tequilas, the juices are extracted with a roller mill and fermented off the fibers while the tahona expression is fermented with the juice and fibers. After fermentation, the must is double distilled to around 56% ABV. The tequila is then proofed using reverse-osmosis water.

Cascahuín

NOM
1123

Region
Los Valles

Distillery
Tequila Cascahuín, El Arenal, Jalisco

Category
100% Blue Agave Tequila

Hydrolysis
Horno

Extraction
Roller Mill or Tahona

Still Type
Stainless Steel Pot Still

Brand Owner
Rosales Family

Blanco

Strength
40% ABV

Price
$$

FLAVOR This tequila offers a lovely aroma of green agave, cut grass, and passionfruit, with sweet notes of cooked agave and fried plantains. On the palate, it has green vegetal flavors such as cut grass, wet stone, and dragon fruit, balanced with sweetness including banana and lemon leaf. If you like grassy and green blancos, then this is worth stocking in your bar.

Tahona Blanco

Strength
42% ABV

Price
$$$

FLAVOR The tequila has strong aromas of fresh cut grass, agave leaves, and light fresh pineapple. The palate starts earthy and oily with notes of roasted gusano (agave moth larva), and it becomes tart and bright like star fruit. Cascahuín's Tahona Blanco is a super earthy and savory tequila. Enjoy this neat with a couple drops of water or as an alternative to sotol in cocktails that call for it.

Cazadores

NOM
1487

Region
Los Altos Sur

Distillery
Bacardi y Compañia, Arandas, Jalisco

Category
100% Blue Agave Tequila

Hydrolysis
Autoclave

Extraction
Diffuser

Still Type
Stainless Steel Pot Still

Brand Owner
Bacardi Limited

Felix Bañuelos founded Cazadores in 1973. Today, the brand's bottles feature an establishment date of 1922, the brand name, and a stag—all selected to honor Bañuelos's grandfather Don Jose Maria Bañuelos. The date refers to the year that Don Jose began making his own tequila and Cazadores, which translates to hunters, refers to Don Jose's long journey to perfecting his homemade tequila recipe, which he subsequently passed down to younger generations. The iconic stag image immortalizes the large buck that once roamed Don Jose's highland agave fields.

The family brand and distillery (NOM 1128) was purchased in 2002 by Bacardi, which moved production to its primary distillery, NOM 1487. Shortly after, Cazadores became one of very few distilleries (at the time) to make its tequila with a diffuser. The closure of the original distillery, El Gallito, must have been disappointing for the Bañuelos family but, not long after its sale to Bacardi, they opened a new distillery, NOM 1412.

Reposado

Strength
40% ABV

Price
$

FLAVOR This tequila has notes of caramel, alcohol, white pepper, and vanilla on the nose. The palate is more complex with sweet caramel, vanilla, and oak flavors. The finish is short, starting sweet and quickly turning bitter and woody. A step up from the blanco, it is ideal for mixing or drinking on the rocks.

Añejo

Strength
40% ABV

Price
$$

FLAVOR This tequila has a strong aroma of caramel and vanilla with a hint of milk chocolate. The palate offers sweet notes of tres leches cake, white pepper, cooked agave, and toasted oak. It finishes hot and sweet with butterscotch, vanilla, and a dry woody note, balancing sweetness with peppery heat. For those who enjoy sweet caramel flavors balanced with some peppery heat, try this on the rocks or with water.

Cazcanes

José Santillán and brothers Colin and Chris Edwards founded Cazcanes in 2015 to celebrate the legacy and heritage of tequila. Colin, a wine maker in Napa, California, traveled to Mexico with Chris to taste tequila and learn how it was made. José, their driver-turned-business-partner, introduced them to several maestros creating great spirits for their local communities. This inspired the trio to create Cazcanes, which is named after the indigenous Caxcan (Kash-Kan) people. Santillán and the Edwardses partnered with Francisco "Don Chico" Jiménez Lazcarro at NOM 1614, where all of their tequilas are made. They begin with organic agave, which are cooked and fermented with a domesticated wild yeast strain. After distillation, the aged tequilas are rested in "reworked and recharred" American oak, also known as STR, barrels. They do not provide the specific amount of time that each tequila is left to mature, stipulating that they are "aged to taste". When the tequila is ready to bottle, the spirit is proofed with spring water collected from the Navichi Springs outside Hostotipaquillo, Jalisco. After proofing, the tequilas are allowed to rest again in stainless steel, which helps the spirit avoid feeling sharp or rough on the tongue.

NOM
1614

Region
Los Valles

Distillery
Tequilera Tap, Amatitán, Jalisco

Category
100% Blue Agave Tequila

Hydrolysis
Low Pressure Autoclave

Extraction
Roller Mill

Still Type
Stainless Steel Pot Still

Brand Owner
Cazcanes Tequila

No. 7 Blanco

Strength
40% ABV

Price
$$$

FLAVOR This tequila offers aromas of lemon curd, baked yam, and lemon blossoms, with evolving floral and vegetal notes. Its flavor profile includes sweet lemon, cooked agave, pepper, ginger, and nutmeg. This is a very nice blanco and is a good choice for those who enjoy cooked agave and citrus flavors. It's a touch hot when neat but it is lovely with a little dilution.

No. 7 Reposado

Strength
40% ABV

Price
$$$$

FLAVOR This reposado offers a light and intriguing aroma of fresh berries and stone fruits, developing into notes of salted caramel and oak. On the palate, it begins soft and smooth with sweet flavors of butterscotch, toffee, and bitter lemon, finishing dry and with pepper, lemon zest, and dry grass. Overall, a delightful, fruit-forward tequila that has good balance between the wood and agave.

No. 9 Blanco

Strength
50% ABV

Price
$$$

FLAVOR This tequila has aromas of wet stone and apricot skins. On the palate, it's smooth with sweet fruit flavors that evolve into earthy notes of dry grass followed by cooked agave, black pepper, and lime zest. If you are a fan of citrusy and vegetal tequilas, this will make you happy, though the higher ABV seems to mask some of the underlying flavors.

No. 10 Blanco Still Strength

Strength
54% ABV

Price
$$$$

FLAVOR This tequila has aromas of wet stone, cottage cheese, and black pepper, evolving to cooked agave and ethanol. It has flavors of baked yams with marshmallows, black pepper, and candied lime, with a silky mouthfeel that becomes aggressive after swallowing. This is an interesting tequila with flavors that go from savory to sweet to vegetal, and is best on the rocks or in cocktails.

Chinaco

NOM
1127

Region
Tamaulipas

Distillery
Tequilera la Gonzaleña, Gonzalez, Tamaulipas

Category
100% Blue Agave Tequila

Hydrolysis
Low Pressure Autoclave

Extraction
Roller Mill

Still Type
Copper Pot Still

Brand Owner
Tequilera La Gonzaleña

Guillermo González Díaz Lombardo (*see* p. 24) created Chinaco in 1972 but was not allowed to sell the spirit as tequila until the Mexican government updated the tequila Norma Oficial Mexicana (NOM) to include 11 municipalities in Tamaulipas. "Chinacos" were celebrated guerrilla cavalryman who fought during the Reform War and the Second Franco-Mexican War in the 1800s, and some troops were led by General Manuel González Flores, the great grandfather of Guillermo.

Tamaulipas sits on the Gulf of Mexico, where blue agaves take on average ten years to mature before they can be harvested. The González family grows more than 60,000 blue agaves on its ranch El Rosillo, 17 miles (28km) northwest of its distillery Tequilera la Gonzaleña. The ranch was first planted with blue agaves in 1966 after a hurricane destroyed much of its cash crops and Sauza (*see* p. 158) indicated that it would purchase the mature agaves. When the deal fell through, the Gonzálezes built their own distillery and began making tequila. In 1983, Chinaco entered the US market and it is widely recognized as the first premium tequila—before Patrón (*see* p. 152), Casa Dragones (*see* p. 80), and many others hit the market, the González family was creating high quality spirits. In 1995, cocktail historian and author David Wondrich wrote that Chinaco was the "Number One Most Influential Spirits Brand of the Last 25 Years" after tasting its Añejo. The brand began to disappear from the US market sometime after 2008 but, at the near end of 2024, the family re-signed with Preiss Imports and it is becoming widely available once more.

Blanco

Strength
40% ABV

Price
$$

FLAVOR This tequila has light aromas of lemon, alcohol, black pepper, and green figs. On the palate, it's light with soft alcohol notes, green agave, and a melon sweetness that resembles a watermelon Jolly Rancher. The finish is semisweet and medium-long, with flavors of candy watermelon and tart strawberry, making it an interesting and potentially polarizing option. It is best enjoyed in cocktails.

Reposado

Strength
40% ABV

Price
$$$

FLAVOR A reposado with bright aromas and flavors of raspberry sorbet, lemon zest, and cooked agave, oak, dry grass, and a juicy acidity. This is a fun and fruity tequila that is very easy to drink. There is a creamy quality that likely comes from the yeast, and it is reminiscent of some mezcals—though the flavors here are more restrained.

Añejo

Strength
40% ABV

Price
$$$

FLAVOR The aroma of this añejo is rich with ripe fruit and oak notes, including orange, nectarine, and papaya. On the palate, it offers a sweet and woody blend of orange, vanilla, peach, oak, fennel seeds, and allspice. This is a beautiful tequila. If you enjoy añejos that are transformed through the interaction of oak and oxygen, this is a tequila you need to try.

Añejo Ultra Cristalino

Strength
40% ABV

Price
$$$

FLAVOR This cristalino offers sweet, cooked agave, papaya, and honey aromas, evolving into vanilla, oak, and tart apple. The palate is very dry with cooked agave, cut grass, vanilla, honey, and white pepper, with fruit notes emerging later. This is a powerful and dry añejo with a lingering finish of green agave and dried mango, best enjoyed neat or with a splash of water.

Enrique Fonseca—the brains behind tequilas such as ArteNOM 1146, Don Fulano, Lapis and more—created Cimarron and introduced it to the US in 2006. At the time, the tequila wasn't labeled as 100% agave, but this was updated in 2010.

Cimarron features a bighorn sheep on its bottles, which fits nicely with the name: Cimarron, when referring to animals, translates as wild or untamed, and some suggest that Fonseca's aim was to create a tequila that embodied this character. The tequila is made from highland-grown agaves that are cooked, crushed, fermented, and distilled at Fonseca's distillery in the city of Tequila. Both spirits are made from a blend of 20% pot- and 80% column-distilled tequilas. Once the blancos are mixed, they are allowed to rest in stainless steel for a few weeks before it is proofed and bottled at 40% ABV. Similarly, the reposado is vatted from the same ratio of tequilas and is aged for four months in American white oak barrels.

Cimarron

NOM
1146

Region
Los Valles

Distillery
La Tequileña, Tequila, Jalisco

Category
100% Blue Agave Tequila

Hydrolysis
Low Pressure Autoclave

Extraction
Screw and Roller Mill

Still Type
Column and Pot Still

Brand Owner
Tequileña

Blanco

Strength
40% ABV

Price
$

FLAVOR This tequila offers a strong aroma of ripe papaya, mineral water, and pepper, with underlying green agave and lime leaves. On the palate, it delivers flavors of cooked agave, papaya, marigolds, white pepper, and chrysanthemum, with a slight gum-numbing sensation. Dollar for dollar, it is hard to beat. It has a great flavor and is super versatile.

Reposado

Strength
40% ABV

Price
$

FLAVOR This tequila has bright, fruity aromas of berries and pineapple, with undertones of lemon zest and caramel. Its soft round palate features cooked agave, lemon zest, light oak, and a hint of sweet mango, with spices balanced by earthy agave fibers. If you enjoy agave-forward reposados but you want something a little lighter for highballs or margaritas, this is a strong contender.

Arturo Lomeli founded Clase Azul in 2000, after a couple of years in the spirits business as a bar owner. In 1997, Lomeli launched a tequila brand called El Teporocho, which came in a painted ceramic bottle of a Mexican bandido with a large sombrero and handlebar mustache. It was a failure. After going back to school to study marketing, however, Lomeli came up with the idea for a more elegant, reusable bottle that evokes the classic Mexican pottery of Talavera—a style of cobalt-blue painted ceramics. Lomeli began by sourcing a reposado tequila from NOM 1137 and, in 2006, he switched to NOM 1416. The Clase Azul bottle had the effect that Lomeli wanted and, despite its high price tag, it became the tequila that people needed to try. In 2021, Clase Azul moved production one more time to NOM 1595, which is owned by Lomeli. The reposado is made from 100% agave and is aged for eight months in American whiskey barrels before being bottled at 40% ABV.

Clase Azul

NOM
1595

Region
Central

Distillery
Casa Tradición, San Agustín, Jalisco

Category
100% Blue Agave Tequila

Hydrolysis
Horno

Extraction
Roller Mill

Still Type
Copper Pot Still

Brand Owner
Clase Azul México

Reposado

Strength
40% ABV

Price
$$$$$

FLAVOR The aroma is overwhelming with notes of vanilla and birthday cake. On the palate, there are competing flavors of sweet vanilla, earthy agave, and oak. The finish is long and sweet with persistent flavors of vanilla frosting and a light touch of lemon zest. Underneath all the vanilla is a decent reposado but it is hard to pick out. For the price, you are mostly paying for the prestige and the bottle than for the liquid. But, if you like vanilla-forward tequilas and want Clase Azul's iconic bottle then it may be worth it. And when the bottle is empty, be sure to reuse it and continue to enjoy its beauty.

Código 1530

A group of golfing buddies and investors including Ron Snyder, former CEO of Crocs, and country singer George Strait, launched Código 1530 in 2016. From the beginning, they knew they wanted their aged tequilas to mature exclusively in French oak. Snyder purchased high-quality wine barrels out of Napa, California, and shipped them to the contract distillery, NOM 1500, in Amatitán, where the tequila was made from valley-grown agaves fermented with bread yeast. Part of the tequila's profile comes from taking wide hearts cut with some heads and tails, which are left in the second distillation to preserve more aroma and flavor compounds. When this is aged for six years, like its XA, it oxidizes and combines with compounds from the barrel to make a more complex spirit.

When Código debuted, it produced a Rosa Tequila, the first modern blanco to rest in red wine barrels with the intent of producing rose-colored tequila. This quickly sparked a trend that several brands, including Calirosa (*see* p. 77) and El Mayor (*see* p. 111), picked up. By 2021, Código was selling in all 50 states of America and 30 countries, so the group built its own distillery, NOM 1616, to meet demand. The following year, Pernod Ricard purchased a majority stake in the company.

NOM
1616

Region
Los Valles

Distillery
Varo Destilería, Amatitán, Jalisco

Category
100% Blue Agave Tequila

Hydrolysis
Low Pressure Autoclave

Extraction
Roller Mill

Still Type
Stainless Steel Pot Still

Brand Owner
Pernod Ricard

Blanco

Strength
40% ABV

Price
$$

FLAVOR This tequila has aromas of fresh papaya, cut grass, and lime oils. On the palate, it's bright with green agave, pepper, and dried papaya notes. The finish is medium to long with flavors of chocolate and orange, making it an elegant tequila for sipping neat or on ice.

Rosa Blanco

Strength
40% ABV

Price
$$

FLAVOR This tequila has a strawberry lemonade-like aroma with notes of green agave, lemon, and black pepper. It offers flavors of cooked agave and dry grass, with a light acidity that makes it bright and enjoyable. The finish is long and dry with hints of oak, raspberries, and green agave, making it a good choice for those who enjoy rosa tequilas on the rocks or in cocktails.

Añejo

Strength
40% ABV

Price
$$$$

FLAVOR Offering aromas of oak, cedar, baking spice, cooked apples, cut grass, lemon zest, and black pepper, this tequila's palate is warm with flavors of cooked agave, green apple, lemon, and white pepper, evolving to earthy notes of dry grass and lime leaf. This is a lovely añejo and a very good example of how oak aging can complement tequila without overpowering it.

Origen Extra Añejo

Strength
40% ABV

Price
$$$$$

FLAVOR This tequila has strong oak, cooked agave, and lemon marmalade aromas, with underlying notes of chocolate, vanilla, and caramel. On the palate, it's warm with flavors of cocoa powder, oak, baked yam, and candied lemon peel, balanced by a slight bitterness. Overall, this is a wood, citrus, and spice-forward XA tequila you should pair with a square of chocolate.

Raul Plascencia created Corazón Tequila in 1998 when he and Cirilo Oropeza built Destiladora San Nicolas (NOM 1440). In 2008, Plascencia sold the distillery to Campari while Corazón was sold to Sazerac. Five years later, production of Corazón tequilas moved to NOM 1103 where it has been produced ever since. True to its name (meaning "heart"), Casa San Matias makes Corazón tequila by taking a very narrow hearts cut during the second distillation. Corazón describes itself as a "single estate" tequila. But in August 2020, CEO Carmen Villareal acknowledged that on any given year they may have to purchase 20–70% of its agaves from third-party farmers. So a more accurate interpretation of the bottle is that all of the spirit inside is made at the Casa San Matias estate, but not all of the agave used to make Corazón is grown at a single estate.

Corazón

NOM
1103

Region
Los Altos Sur

Distillery
Tequila San Matías de Jalisco, Ojo de Agua de Latillas, Jalisco

Category
100% Blue Agave Tequila

Hydrolysis
Horno

Extraction
Roller Mill

Still Type
Stainless Steel Pot Still

Brand Owner
Sazerac Company

Single Estate Blanco

Strength
40% ABV

Price
$

FLAVOR This blanco tequila has an aroma of bitter orange, green anise, pineapple, and lemon. On the palate, it's dry and warm with sweet orange, dry lemon zest, black pepper, and shishito pepper notes. The finish is semidry with lingering orange and grass flavors, making it a fun, orange-forward, and slightly spicy tequila.

Single Estate Reposado

Strength
40% ABV

Price
$

FLAVOR There are light, evolving aromas of pears, mineral water, and floral notes such as sweet pinot grigio. On the palate, it begins with a big floral note, followed by blackcurrant, dry, bitter lime peel, and a light oak character. This reposado is very floral and fruity which makes it a nice departure from all of the aged tequilas driven by oak and vanilla.

Single Estate Añejo

Strength
40% ABV

Price
$$

FLAVOR This tequila offers bright, fruity aromas of green apple and strawberry-flavored marshmallows. The palate continues with strong mixed berry, Fuyu persimmon, and mandarin orange flavors, balanced by oak and vanilla. The finish is dry, fruity, and lightly oaky, making it a fun "non-traditional" and versatile añejo great for sipping neat.

Single Estate Extra Añejo

Strength
40% ABV

Price
$$$

FLAVOR This tequila has earthy, sweet, and citrusy aromas with a distinct whiskey character. On the palate, it's bright and warm with flavors of cooked agave, oak, lemon zest, and a developing fruitiness similar to dried peach. This is not the most complex tequila on the market, but for its price there is plenty to enjoy. Overall, a versatile XA, especially for bourbon drinkers exploring tequila.

Corralejo

NOM
1368

Region
Guanajuato

Distillery
Tequilera Corralejo, Abasolo, Guanajuato

Category
100% Blue Agave Tequila

Hydrolysis
Horno

Extraction
Roller Mill

Still Type
Column and Pot Still

Brand Owner
Fraternity Spirits

In 1996, Leonardo Rodriguez Moreno created Tequila Corralejo and within a year began selling it in the US. Corralejo is unique because it is one of very few tequilas made outside of Jalisco and is distilled at Hacienda Corralejo, the birthplace of Miguel Hidalgo y Costilla: the "father of Mexican Independence." Hacienda Corralejo was founded around 1565 by Don Alonso de Angulo y Montesino and, for the next 200 years, it was used for raising sheep, cattle, and breeding horses. Tequila Corralejo claims the hacienda was the first commercial producer of tequila in 1755. Records from neighboring haciendas do list large agave plantations and indicate that seasonal tenants would pay to set up a temporary distillery to produce small amounts of mezcal, but there are no records like this for Hacienda Corralejo. Also, the name tequila wasn't used for agave spirits until 1854 and only applied to mezcal made around the town of Tequila. However, in 1994 when Rodriguez Moreno purchased the hacienda, the boundaries set by tequila's denomination of origin had expanded to include it and other municipalities in Guanajuato. In addition to a distillery, Rodriguez Moreno has revitalized the hacienda with the construction of a museum and a glass factory to make bottles for his tequila. Since the brand's inception, Corralejo tequila has been sold in its custom 15in- (38cm-) tall bottle which is a physical symbol of its motto: "Those with Pride Stand Tall".

Silver

Strength
40% ABV

Price
$

FLAVOR This tequila offers aromas of cooked agave, caramel, and pineapple, with a hint of green agave. On the palate, it's semidry with notes of white pepper, earth, and light caramel sweetness. The spirit finishes dry with notes of agave fibers and ripe pineapple. A good tequila for mixing and cocktails.

Reposado

Strength
40% ABV

Price
$

FLAVOR This tequila offers light oak, caramel, and sour fruit aromas. The palate is semidry with notes of bourbon, maraschino, sweet lemon, and cooked agave. It has a medium-long finish of sweet orange, making this a light and easy tequila that has enough complexity to be enjoyed on the rocks or in cocktails.

Añejo

Strength
40% ABV

Price
$$

FLAVOR This añejo has a lightly funky, earthy aroma with notes of paprika, panela, and dark chocolate. The palate is earthy and oaky with burnt sugar and vanilla, leading to a long finish with oak and burnt sugar. It's an interesting añejo, suitable for cocktails like an Old Fashioned (*see* p. 187) or Manhattan.

Extra Añejo

Strength
40% ABV

Price
$$$

FLAVOR This tequila offers aromas of dark chocolate, orange peel, oak, berries, and earth. The palate is spicy like rye whiskey and star anise. It resembles a Sazerac cocktail followed by notes of agave, tropical fruit, and semidark chocolate. The finish is long and semidry with fading oak and earthy notes, making it unique for those who prefer less dessert-like extra añejos.

Cuervo Tradicional

In the 1970s, Cuervo Especial (*see* p. 132), a mixto tequila, exploded in popularity and it seems likely that Casa Cuervo created the Tradicional line as the 100% agave brand to compete with Herradura (*see* pp. 128–129). TTB's Public COLA Registry shows the first labels for Cuervo Tradicional were approved for use in the United States in the fall of 1988. According to Cuervo, its Tradicional Blanco is made to mimic how tequila would have been made in 1795—however, at that time the drink would have tasted more like mezcal than what we know as tequila today. Interestingly, the original back label suggested that the reposado should be enjoyed straight from the freezer, which reflects a different attitude to the way in which premium spirits should be consumed.

The line remained unchanged for the next 30 years until the release of Tradicional Añejo in 2020. In addition to aging the tequila for at least 12 months in new high-char American oak barrels, it is finished for another two to four months in Bushmills Irish single malt whiskey barrels. In 2022, Cuervo added a cristalino to the line; it is made from a blend of reposado and XA tequilas.

NOM
1122

Region
Los Valles

Distillery
La Rojeña, Tequila, Jalisco

Category
100% Blue Agave Tequila

Hydrolysis
Horno

Extraction
Roller Mill

Still Type
Copper Pot Still

Brand Owner
Casa Cuervo

Blanco

Strength
40% ABV

Price
$

FLAVOR This tequila offers light aromas of cooked agave, lemon meringue, and subtle vegetal notes. The palate is consistently sweet with cooked agave, then becomes spicy with lemon pith and pepper. It finishes medium-long and dry with lemon zest and birchwood, making it a pleasant and soft blanco suitable for neat sipping or cocktails.

Reposado

Strength
40% ABV

Price
$

FLAVOR This tequila has a nose with green agave, citrus, honey, cooked yam, and pepper, evolving to plum, oak, vanilla, cantaloupe, and black pepper. On the palate, it starts sweet with cooked agave, then becomes dry with lemon zest, white pepper, and oak, building with baked yam and dry agave fibers. This is an easy tequila to recommend for those just getting into the spirit.

Cristalino Reposado

Strength
40% ABV

Price
$$

FLAVOR This tequila has aromas of ethanol, oak, lemon zest, and tart blackberries. On the palate, it is lightly sweet with flavors of strawberry, banana, papaya, pepper, and lime zest. The finish is long and dry with lingering fruity notes, making it a good choice for fruity cocktails.

Añejo

Strength
40% ABV

Price
$$

FLAVOR This añejo tequila offers aromas of raspberries, strawberries, dried plums, nutmeg, sweet paprika, raisins, and oak. The flavor matches the aroma, with an initial sharpness that fades to persistent dried fruit and oak notes. It's a well-priced, sweet, and dry fruity añejo, suitable for drinking neat, though there is no discernable impact from the Irish single malt whiskey finish.

Cutwater

NOM
1110

Region
Los Valles

Distillery
Tequila Orendain de Jalisco, Tequila, Jalisco

Category
100% Blue Agave Tequila

Hydrolysis
Horno

Extraction
Roller Mill

Still Type
Copper and Stainless Steel Still

Brand Owner
Anheuser-Busch

In 2014 Yuseff Cherney, the then co-founder of Ballast Point Brewing and Spirits, was teaching brewing classes at the University of California San Diego, when he met a student whose family owned NOM 1110 in the city of Tequila. Over the next five years, Cherney, who had dreamed of creating his own tequila, maintained his relationship with the Orendain family which helped inform the development of Cutwater tequila later on. In 2015, Constellation Brands purchased the brewery and two years later Cherney and Earl Kight, a Ballast colleague, founded Cutwater Spirits.

Cutwater Spirits released its first blanco tequila in October 2019, just eight months after Anheuser-Busch purchased the San Diego-based company. Cutwater named its tequila Rayador, which is the Spanish name for the black skimmer bird. This followed a tradition from Cherney's Ballast Point days where each product was named after an animal or place found in San Diego. But, shortly after Anheuser-Busch acquired Cutwater, it dropped the name from the label, though it made the skull of the black skimmer more prominent. All of its aged tequilas are rested in Cutwater whiskey barrels (the brand produces a range of spirits alongside its tequila) that are specially shipped from San Diego, California, to Tequila, Jalisco. Aging tequila in Cutwater barrels creates a signature profile that has attracted the attention of the wider spirits world. In 2021, Cutwater Reposado earned a Gold Medal at the American Distilling Institute's International Spirit Competition and was named Best Tequila and Best International Agave Spirit of the Year.

Blanco

Strength
40% ABV

Price
$

FLAVOR This tequila offers a lightly sweet aroma of cooked agave and apricots, with hints of dark cherries, grass, and lemon as it breathes. On the palate, it has a light fruity sweetness of banana and pineapple, balanced by vegetal and slightly bitter lime. This is a well-priced and good all-around tequila, making it ideal if you enjoy a balance of fruit, citrus, and agave.

Reposado

Strength
40% ABV

Price
$$

FLAVOR This tequila offers a lightly sweet aroma of cooked agave and apricots, with hints of dark cherries, grass, and lemon as it breathes. On the palate, it has a light fruity sweetness of banana and pineapple, balanced by vegetal and slightly bitter lime. This is a well-priced and good all-around tequila making it ideal if you enjoy a balance of fruit, citrus, and agave.

Añejo

Strength
40% ABV

Price
$$

FLAVOR This añejo offers bright green and citrus aromas, with deeper notes of cooked agave, dark cherries, and caramel. On the palate, it's energetic with green flavors, oak, maltiness, and cooked agave. This is an oak-forward añejo and the malt character makes it a unique and enjoyable spirit to drink. Try it neat or use it as a substitute in whiskey-based cocktails.

Extra Añejo

Strength
40% ABV

Price
$$$$

FLAVOR This tequila offers aromas of green agave, black pepper, dried mango, lime zest, and green apple, with a bright, warm palate of baked yam, vanilla, caramel apple, and distinct American single malt whiskey note. The finish is long and semidry, featuring green apple, oak, limeade, malt whiskey, and cooked agave. This unique tequila is recommended for fans of ASMW or those who prefer floral and citrusy XAs.

American entrepreneur Brent Hocking launched DeLeón Tequila on Cinco de Mayo 2009. Hocking initially announced that DeLeón would be a limited annual release in select cities such as Los Angeles, New York, Las Vegas, Miami, Hong Kong, Dubai, Macau, San Tropez, and Monte Carlo. From 2008 to 2014, Hocking sourced the tequila from NOM 1519 in Guanajuato beginning with a blanco and reposado, and evolving to include an añejo and extra añejo in 2010. In 2014, Diageo and Sean Combs purchased the DeLeón brand as a joint venture and moved its production to NOM 1535 where it has remained since. Ten years later, in 2024, Diageo bought out Combs's ownership stake in the brand, making the UK company the sole owner of DeLeón. Today, DeLeón tequila is fermented with champagne yeast and both the reposado and añejo are aged in American oak and French wine barrels.

DeLeón

NOM
1535

Region
Los Altos Sur

Distillery
Destilería Morales, Arandas, Jalisco

Category
100% Blue Agave Tequila

Hydrolysis
Horno

Extraction
Roller Mill

Still Type
Stainless Steel Pot Still

Brand Owner
Diageo

Reposado

Strength
40% ABV

Price
$$

FLAVOR This tequila offers a pleasant aroma of cooked agave and oak, evolving into lemon zest, blackberry, and caramel notes. On the palate, it presents a light sharpness followed by flavors of lemon curd, vanilla, caramel, oak, cooked agave, lime juice, and earthy agave fibers. Overall, it's a decent tequila with nice flavors that don't seem to have been manipulated after distillation.

Añejo

Strength
40% ABV

Price
$$

FLAVOR This tequila offers aromas of vanilla, candied orange, and caramel. On the palate, it's sweet with lemon, vanilla, cooked agave, and oak flavors that intensify with each sip. The tequila has a mouthwatering juiciness to it and the acidity provides balance in what might otherwise be a vanilla dominant añejo.

Divertido

Verde Tequila, by the De Anda Orozco family of 4 Copas (*see* pp. 66–67), created Divertido in 2023 in partnership with master distiller Iliana Partida at NOM 1522. Divertido translates as "fun" and, while it's not organic like 4 Copas, it is crafted as a premium tequila with the same high standards and attention to detail. Divertido's agaves are cooked in an autoclave and, after distillation, the blanco is filtered twice and then bottled. The aged expressions are rested in used whiskey barrels made of American oak.

Blanco

Strength
40% ABV

Price
$$

FLAVOR This tequila offers aromas of tart plum skins, wet stone, white pepper, and baked yam. The initial taste includes strawberry bubblegum, pepper, cooked agave, sweet lemon, dried apricots, and dry grass, evolving into richer cooked berries, chocolate blueberries, and dark cherries. The finish is semisweet and medium-long with lasting berry and papaya flavors, making it a fun and enjoyable tequila.

Reposado

Strength
40% ABV

Price
$$

FLAVOR This tequila offers aromas of cooked agave, papaya, vanilla, oak, and red grapes. On the palate, it has sweet flavors of vanilla, lemon zest, and cooked agave, evolving to caramel, bitter oak, and unripe pear. The finish is long and semidry with notes of dark chocolate, oak, cooked agave, and an earthy vegetal note. Overall, a nice fruit- and oak-forward reposado.

NOM
1522

Region
Los Valles

Distillery
Hacienda de Oro, Amatitán, Jalisco

Category
100% Blue Agave Tequila

Hydrolysis
Autoclave

Extraction
Roller Mill

Still Type
Copper Pot Still

Brand Owner
Verde Tequila

Enrique Fonseca (of Cimarron tequila—*see* p. 90) and his nephew Sergio Mendoza co-founded Don Fulano in December 2002. The brand name translates as a "gentleman of unknown identity," which was inspired by the maxim, "He who knows does not speak. He who speaks does not know." Fonseca and Mendoza are fourth- and fifth-generation agave growers and all the agaves used in Don Fulano tequila come from their estate in the highlands of Jalisco, outside Atotonilco. The pair select only agaves with the highest maturity, known as "maduro" and "pinto," for harvesting and, after cooking the majority of the must is fermented in open-air stainless steel fermenters without fibers and a smaller portion is open-air fermented with fibers. The musts are either double-distilled in copper pots or column-distilled. These separate batches of tequila are then blended (80% pot, 20% column) for blancos or aged separately in French wine barrels made of Nevers and Limousin oak.

Don Fulano

NOM
1146

Region
Los Valles

Distillery
La Tequileña, Tequila, Jalisco

Category
100% Blue Agave Tequila

Hydrolysis
Low Pressure Autoclave

Extraction
Screw and Roller Mill

Still Type
Column and Pot Still

Brand Owner
Mendoza-Fonseca family

Blanco

Strength
40% ABV

Price
$$

FLAVOR The tequila has a sweet and sour, fruity aroma with notes of strawberry and bubblegum, followed by floral undertones. On the palate, it's full and semisweet with savory cooked agave, fresh fennel, and lime jelly flavors. The long, semisweet finish features sweet lime and dry agave fibers, which invite another sip. If you enjoy cooked agave in your blanco, give this a try.

Blanco Fuerte

Strength
50% ABV

Price
$$$

FLAVOR This fuerte (which means strong) has notes of cooked agave, papaya, pepper, and lemon zest, with a creamy yogurt-like aroma. On the palate, it delivers warm cinnamon spice with sweet, cooked agave—a signature of NOM 1146. The long, semidry finish features lingering flavors of strawberry, sweet cream, and cooked agave, making it a strong yet smooth tequila ideal for making cocktails with a kick.

Reposado

Strength
40% ABV

Price
$$$

FLAVOR This tequila offers a light, inviting nose with vanilla, green agave, guava, and sweet cherry notes. The palate is naturally sweet, balanced with oak and pepper, featuring vanilla, cooked agave, cherries, sweet cinnamon, and lime zest. The finish is semidry, with flavors of cooked agave, baking chocolate, and a hint of white pepper, making it an expertly balanced and elegant reposado that is hard to beat.

Añejo

Strength
40% ABV

Price
$$$

FLAVOR The tequila has an aroma of cooked yam, green agave, and subtle cinnamon with hints of fruit. On the palate, it's warm and dry, offering flavors of cinnamon, oak, and fruits such as banana and pineapple that evolve into spiced banana bread. There is also a savoriness that resembles sake kasu. If you enjoy rich and savory añejos that aren't covered up with oak and vanilla, then you need to try this excellent tequila.

Imperial Extra Añejo

Strength
40% ABV

Price
$$$$$

FLAVOR This tequila offers a rich and spicy aroma with citrus, caramel, and gentian notes. On the palate, it bursts with flavors of cherry, nutmeg, sweet orange, vanilla, chocolate, and oak, balanced by green agave and black pepper. This is testament to the skill and knowledge of Enrique Fonseca and why he is one of the very best when it comes to long-aged tequila.

In 1942, 17-year-old Don Julio González-Frausto Estrada secured a loan and began making tequila to support his family. He started construction on a new distillery called La Primavera in Atotonilco el Alto, Jalisco, in 1974. For six decades, Don Julio and his sons ran a successful business selling a mixto called Tres Magueyes. In 1985 the sons created a batch of 100% agave tequila to celebrate their father's 60th birthday. Everyone enjoyed the tequila so much that they decided to launch Don Julio Tequila as a brand two years later. In May 1999, the family sold its majority share to Seagram & Sons, but just seven months later Seagram collapsed and Don Julio ended up with Diageo. From 2003 to 2014, Diageo and Casa Cuervo ran Don Julio as a joint venture but then Diageo ended the partnership and gained full ownership of Don Julio, while selling its Bushmills Distillery to Cuervo. Its reposado, añejo, and extra añejo are aged in American white oak barrels for 8, 18, and 36 months respectively.

Don Julio

NOM
1449

Region
Ciénega

Distillery
Diageo México Operaciones, Atotonilco el Alto, Jalisco

Category
100% Blue Agave Tequila

Hydrolysis
Horno

Extraction
Roller Mill

Still Type
Stainless Steel Pot Still

Brand Owner
Diageo

Blanco

Strength
40% ABV

Price
$$

FLAVOR This tequila has light aromas of green agave, lemon, and vanilla, which evolve into orange blossom. The palate is sweet then slightly bitter with pineapple, agave fibers, and wet stone, becoming sweeter with cooked agave and white pepper. It's a simple and enjoyable blanco if you are new to tequila. Recommended for mixing, cocktails, or shots.

Reposado

Strength
40% ABV

Price
$$

FLAVOR This tequila offers aromas of caramel, dark brown sugar, chocolate brownies, and sweet pineapple, with initial sweet flavors of caramel and vanilla. It transitions to a slight dryness with oak and pineapple, then returns to notes of fudge brownie and cooked agave. This makes a good "dessert tequila" and is best served straight from the freezer.

Añejo

Strength
40% ABV

Price
$$$

FLAVOR This añejo has earthy, vanilla, caramel, and oak aromas, which become nuttier over time. The palate offers a mix of sweet and dry flavors such as vanilla, raw almonds, lemonade, and oak. With subsequent sips the nut and baking spices flavors intensify and reveal Fuyu persimmon. Overall, a sweeter vanilla-forward añejo but with interesting layers of nuts, fruit, and oak.

70 Cristalino Añejo

Strength
40% ABV

Price
$$$

FLAVOR This spirit offers vanilla, oak, and fruit aromas, reminiscent of a VSOP Cognac or a high-rye bourbon. The palate is bitter and acrid with vanilla, stone fruit, and oak flavors. The finish is short and aggressive with a general woodiness. It's recommended for bourbon fans, since it lacks agave character and tastes similar to a clarified version of Bulleit Bourbon.

1942 Extra Añejo

Strength
40% ABV

Price
$$$$

FLAVOR This tequila has a soft aroma of lemon zest, white pepper, baked yam, and oak that is dominated by vanilla. On the palate, it's sweet and slightly acrid, featuring vanilla, persimmon, cashews, oak, and bitter lemon flavors. The finish is long and semidry with lingering bitter lemon, young oak, and caramel, fading to agave fibers, malt extract, and birchwood. Taste it first before buying a full bottle.

Richard Sorenson founded Dulce Vida in 2008, and it is one of few tequila brands that is certified as organic. With a background in finance and technology, Sorenson made his move to the world of tequila following a short stint as COO of an organic drinks company. Since Dulce Vida's launch, the tequila has been made at a number of distilleries in Jalisco and one in Michoacán. Today, Carlos Jurado distills Dulce Vida Organic Tequila at NOM 1443 in the highlands west of Aranda. Unlike other tequila brands that bottle at 40% ABV, Dulce Vida launched its blanco, reposado and añejo at 50% and only later offered a lower strength version. In 2014, Dulce Vida celebrated its fifth anniversary with the first release of an extra añejo, which is aged for five years in Napa Valley red wine barrels instead of the ex-bourbon barrels used for its reposado and añejo. In May 2016, Eric Dopkins and Chad Auler, former executives of Deep Eddy Vodka, purchased Dulce Vida through their company Milestone Brands.

Dulce Vida

NOM
1443

Region
Los Altos Sur

Distillery
Grupo Industrial Tequilero de Los Altos de Jalisco, San Ignacio Cerro Gordo, Jalisco

Category
100% Blue Agave Tequila

Hydrolysis
High Pressure Autoclave

Extraction
Roller Mill

Still Type
Stainless Steel Pot Still

Brand Owner
Milestone Brands

Organic Blanco

Strength
40% ABV

Price
$

FLAVOR This blanco has a vibrant aroma of fresh orange juice, cooked agave, and yams. On the palate, it offers a pleasant blend of sweet fruit notes, cooked agave, and earthiness. This tequila is a great entry-level option for cocktails, though it lacks complexity for sipping neat.

Organic 100 Proof Blanco

Strength
50% ABV

Price
$$

FLAVOR The 100 Proof Blanco has earthy, orange, cornmeal, and ethanol aromas. On the palate, it offers sweet and roasted flavors of cooked agave, caramel, and milk chocolate, with a smooth alcohol presence. While there is no oak, someone used to drinking higher proof whiskeys and who has a bit of a sweet tooth will likely enjoy the flavors in this blanco.

Organic Reposado

Strength
40% ABV

Price
$

FLAVOR This tequila has light aromas of lemon zest, white pepper, cooked agave, ripe plums, and vanilla. On the palate, it's earthy and sweet with flavors of cooked agave, lime zest, dry mango and vanilla. The finish is medium, dry, and complex with notes of grass, agave, and plum skins. This is a decent reposado but bitterness builds on the tongue as you drink it neat.

Organic 100 Proof Reposado

Strength
50% ABV

Price
$$

FLAVOR This spirit features aromas of lemon zest, vanilla, oak, plum, and apricot. On the palate, it's soft with flavors of cooked agave, raisins, plums, vanilla, grass, and oak. The added alcohol enhances some of the sweet fruit flavors and not the oak. The finish is long and semisweet, making it a powerful yet balanced option.

Organic 100 Proof Extra Añejo

Strength
50% ABV

Price
$$$$

FLAVOR This tequila offers tart berry and oak aromas, with a hot palate featuring strong vanilla, caramel, and fruit flavors, resembling a VSOP Cognac. Dominant tannins add a drying sensation that leads to a long, semisweet finish with notes of grass, green agave, key lime, and green apple. I'd recommend this XA for brandy drinkers or those seeking a fruity, oak-forward aged tequila. It's best enjoyed with a splash of water or ice due to its higher proof.

For more than seven decades, the family of Luis Ángel Villalobos has been growing agaves around the town of Romita, Guanajuato. In 2000, Villalobos successfully petitioned the CRT (tequila regulators) to expand the denomination of origin to include their village so they and neighboring farmers could use or sell agaves to make tequila. Villalobos built a distillery in Aranda, Jalisco, to make El Ateo tequila, which means it is one of very few single brand NOMs. Back in Romita, ripe agaves upwards of 39°Brix (sugar content), are harvested from the family estate and trucked to the distillery. After the agaves are cooked and crushed, the must is fermented by wild yeast and double distilled. The blanco is then proofed with well water and aerated before bottling to help soften the spirit. El Alteo's aged expressions, the reposado and añejo, are aged in ex-bourbon barrels for six months and fourteen months respectively.

El Ateo

NOM
1635

Region
Los Altos Sur

Distillery
Plantaciones Tequilana, Arandas, Jalisco

Category
100% Blue Agave Tequila

Hydrolysis
Horno

Extraction
Tahona

Still Type
Stainless Steel Pot Still

Brand Owner
Plantaciones Tequilana

Blanco

Strength
40% ABV

Price
$$

FLAVOR This tequila offers aromas of black pepper, green agave, lemon zest, and baked yam. On the palate, it has flavors of cooked agave, brown sugar, lemon juice, and white pepper, with increasing citrus and alcohol intensity. This is a breakout spirit and an excellent tequila that should be tried by any fan of citrus, green agave, and pepper in their blancos.

Reposado

Strength
40% ABV

Price
$$

FLAVOR This reposado offers a lovely aroma of lime zest, marigolds, white pepper, honey, and toasted oak. Its flavor starts citrusy, then develops into a spicy character with notes of cinnamon, cardamom, and cedar, complemented by cooked agave and vanilla. This is a lovely reposado and worth picking up if you are a fan of the tequilas from Enrique Fonseca (NOM 1146) (*see* pp. 71, 90, 104, 121, 137, 154, and 166).

In 1998, Paul Lux—founder of the St. Louis-based Luxco liquor company—partnered with the Gonzalez family to create El Mayor, a high quality tequila made in the Tequila valley. By 2017, the partnership had proved a success and the Gonzalezes and Luxco built Destiladora Gonzalez Lux (NOM 1603) in Arandas as the new home of El Mayor. Rodolfo Gonzalez, a third-generation distiller, has overseen all production at NOM 1603 from the beginning, and his daughter Graciela Gonzalez serves as the brand's ambassador. Despite moving its distillery to the highlands, El Mayor still uses valley-grown agaves to produce its tequilas. After distillation, the tequila is either bottled as a blanco or rested in ex-bourbon barrels for the majority of its aged expressions. The one difference is its Rosado, which is aged for nine months in Cabernet Sauvignon wine casks from Napa Valley, California.

El Mayor

NOM
1603

Region
Los Altos Sur

Distillery
Destiladora González Lux, Arandas, Jalisco

Category
100% Blue Agave Tequila

Hydrolysis
Low Pressure Autoclave

Extraction
Roller Mill

Still Type
Stainless Steel Pot Still

Brand Owner
Luxco

Blanco

Strength
40% ABV

Price
$

FLAVOR This tequila offers bright aromas of green agave, pineapple, apricot, and white pepper, with underlying strawberry and cooked agave. On the palate, it provides sweet orange and lemon, cooked agave, and dried papaya, with a slight fading warmth. Overall, an excellent blanco with enough complexity to enjoy any way you like. Hard to beat for the price.

Reposado

Strength
40% ABV

Price
$

FLAVOR The reposado offers pleasant aromas of cooked agave, vanilla, and caramel, with subtle hints of lime, pepper, and pineapple. On the palate, it features cooked agave, plum, dry mango, and barrel flavors such as caramel and vanilla, balanced by green agave and a light pepper spice. A solid workhorse tequila that's best enjoyed on the rocks or in cocktails due to its slight sharpness if sipped neat.

Rosado Reposado

Strength
40% ABV

Price
$$

FLAVOR This tequila has a light, bright, and fruity aroma, reminiscent of rosé wine with toasted oak notes. On the palate, it offers sweet jammy fruit flavors, cooked agave, subtle oak, and a hint of vanilla. The finish is dry with lingering notes of stewed strawberries, toasted oak, and clove, making it a good entry tequila for wine lovers. Try it in a spritz with a slice of grapefruit.

Añejo

Strength
40% ABV

Price
$

FLAVOR This tequila offers inviting aromas of orange zest, cooked agave, white pepper, oak, and honey, evolving to include tanned leather. The palate is sweet with bright fruit flavors of blackberries, oak, nutmeg, cooked agave, and ripe persimmon. This is a luxurious añejo at a bafflingly low price that shows great balance between the agave and barrel flavors.

Cristalino Añejo

Strength
40% ABV

Price
$$

FLAVOR The tequila offers light, sweet aromas of anise, cut grass, oak, and vanilla. On the palate, it's soft with subtle fruit and licorice, evolving to lime zest, cooked agave, and white pepper that warms the tongue. A very nice example of an añejo cristalino. The flavors make sense and there is a subtlety to the spirit that likely comes from the filtration process.

Don Jorge Salles Cuervo, a descendant of the famed Cuervo family, founded El Tequileño in 1959. He chose the name as an homage to the town of Tequila, but although the distillery is in Tequila, the family sources their agaves from the highlands. In 1964, when the Norma codified the use of non-agave sugars in tequila, Don Jorge—like many others of his time—began making a mixto tequila. During this process, the juices are extracted from cooked agaves and mixed with sugar. Rather than use refined white sugar, Don Jorge chose to use piloncillo, a form of unrefined cane sugar made by boiling sugarcane juice to evaporate the water. The mixture is then fermented in open cement tanks. The quality of the tequila attracted the attention of Javier Delgado Corona, owner of the Cantina La Capilla—a legendary bar in the center of Tequila. Javier chose to use El Tequileño Blanco for his new cocktail, the Batanga, which was made with tequila, cola, and lime, and helped cement El Tequileño's reputation.

El Tequileño

NOM
1108

Region
Los Valles

Distillery
Jorge Salles Cuervo y Sucesores, Tequila, Jalisco

Category
Mixto Tequila (70% Blue Agave, 30% Piloncillo)

Hydrolysis
High Pressure Autoclave

Extraction
Roller Mill

Still Type
Copper Pot Still

Brand Owner
Paradise Spirits

Blanco

Strength
40% ABV

Price
$

FLAVOR This tequila has a pleasant aroma and tastes of pineapple, passionfruit, and orange blossoms, though it is slightly dryer and less juicy on the tongue. There are also underlying notes of cooked agave and grass. This blanco is an almost perfectly executed mixto, proving quality is about intention and execution, not just the percentage of agave. This affordable and versatile tequila is worth picking up.

Reposado

Strength
40% ABV

Price
$

FLAVOR This tequila offers bright aromas of lemon, lime, and green agave. On the palate, it's light, sweet, and dry, with tropical fruit flavors such as mango, papaya, and guava, supported by oak and dry grass. The finish is long and dry with a nice lime acidity that keeps you coming back. This is a fantastic mixto that puts many 100% agave tequilas to shame.

El Tequileño (100% Agave)

Years later, Don Jorge Salles Cuervo's son Juan Antonio took over operation of the distillery and now his grandson Jorge Antonio "Tony" serves as its master distiller. To produce its 100% agave tequilas, highland agaves are cooked in autoclaves the family built from repurposed railcars and are fermented with the same yeast strain started by Don Jorge back in 1959. The blanco comes off the still at 50% ABV and is trucked to the bottling and aging facility in Guadalajara. One of El Tequileño's signatures is that all its tequilas spend some time in oak to mellow before bottling. Its blancos are rested for 14 days, while its reposados are aged for three to eight months. The añejo spends 18 months in American and French oak and has a small amount of extra añejo blended in. And, lastly, its Reposado Rare is aged for six years in oak barrels that hold more than 600l (158 US gallons), which is why it cannot be labeled as an extra añejo. For many years, El Tequileño was known as Mexico's best-kept secret but, in 2017, that began to change when Paradise Spirits purchased the brand and distillery. Part of the agreement with Paradise was that the Salles family would continue to make El Tequileño with the same methods Don Jorge developed more than 60 years earlier.

NOM
1108

Region
Los Valles

Distillery
Jorge Salles Cuervo y Sucesores, Tequila, Jalisco

Category
100% Blue Agave Tequila

Hydrolysis
High Pressure Autoclave

Extraction
Roller Mill

Still Type
Copper Pot Still

Brand Owner
Paradise Spirits

Platinum Still Strength

Strength
50% ABV

Price
$$$

FLAVOR The high-proof blanco features aromas of wet stone, lemongrass, and cooked agave, with a pleasant funky fruit flavor and more tropical fruit and tart lime flavors with each sip. This is a nice example of a high proof blanco where the higher ABV adds a natural sweetness to the spirit and helps balance the agave, fruit, and bitter lime flavors.

Reposado Gran Reserva

Strength
40% ABV

Price
$$

FLAVOR This tequila offers a soft and lovely aroma of sweet lemon, green agave, stone fruit, and oak. The palate explodes with orchard fruits, such as apricots and nectarines, balanced by dryer oak and agave flavors. The finish is long, semisweet, and fruity, making it an expertly crafted, well-balanced and thoroughly enjoyable tequila worth searching out.

Cristalino Reposado

Strength
40% ABV

Price
$$

FLAVOR The tequila has a light aroma of lime zest, pepper, pineapple, and coconut, with a sweet cooked agave note. On the palate, it's fruity with strawberry, honeydew, lemon, and mango flavors, balanced by dry grass, green agave, and oak. This is a lovely cristalino that retains all the best elements of an aged tequila but without the color.

Reposado Rare

Strength
40% ABV

Price
$$$$$

FLAVOR This tequila has a prominent oak aroma, balanced by orchard fruits and agave. The flavor profile features wonderful orange notes, ranging from blossoms, zest, and honey, with subtle oak, wood spices, and a light lemon acidity all on a bed of cooked agave and subtle caramel. The finish is medium-long and semidry, with hints of dried fruit, tobacco, and oak, making it a beautiful spirit you need to try if you enjoy fruity, oak-forward tequilas.

In the late 1980s, Robert Denton, Marilyn Smith, and the Camarena family created El Tesoro de Don Felipe as a small batch tequila brand focused purely on quality. El Tesoro, which translates as "the treasure," is made at the same distillery (NOM 1139) that Don Felipe Camarena founded in 1937. In 1999, Denton and Smith sold their trademark for El Tesoro to Fortune Brands which over the years has morphed from Beam Inc to Beam Suntory, and now Suntory Global Spirits. Today, Don Felipe's grandson Carlos Camarena is the master distiller, and his sister Jenny Camarena is head of operations for both El Tesoro and Tapatio (*see* p. 163). In addition to crushing its cooked agaves with a tahona, El Tesoro also ferments its must with the agave fibers in open-air wooden tanks. All of El Tesoro's tequilas are then distilled to proof, which is uncommon for tequila. The blanco is distilled to 40% ABV and then bottled while its aged tequilas rest in ex-bourbon barrels for between nine and eleven months for its reposado and two to three years for its añejo.

El Tesoro

NOM
1139

Region
Los Altos Sur

Distillery
La Alteña, Arandas, Jalisco

Category
100% Blue Agave Tequila

Hydrolysis
Horno

Extraction
Tahona

Still Type
Copper Pot Still

Brand Owner
Suntory Global Spirits

Blanco

Strength
40% ABV

Price
$$

FLAVOR This tequila has a bright nose with aromas of green agave, cut grass, and lemon zest. On the palate, it offers flavors of pepper, cooked agave, lemon zest, and agave fibers, ending with a light sweetness. This is an elegant blanco that should be enjoyed neat or with a small splash of water.

Añejo

Strength
40% ABV

Price
$$$

FLAVOR A tequila with an inviting aroma of cooked agave, oak, vanilla, and white pepper. On the palate, there is a light vanilla sweetness as well as soft tannins followed by bright lime and vegetal notes. The finish is long, semidry, and soft, with flavors of cooked agave, agave fibers, and oak. This is a great añejo that expertly marries the agave and oak barrel into a lovely spirit.

El Viejito

Indalecio Núñez Muro founded Tequila el Viejito (Via HeToe) in 1937, making it the first distillery in Atotonilco. It first entered the US market in 1980 but, for about 30 years, it was only available for sale in Mexico. Then, in 2023, Juan Eduardo Núñez brought it back and the spirit is starting to gain attention once again. El Viejito is one of the few historic tequila brands that is still owned by the family that started the company. The distillery itself is run by Karina Rojo, who serves as the master distiller and distillery manager. It is under her watchful eye that the highland agaves are cooked, milled, fermented, and distilled. El Viejito's blancos are proofed with deep well water and its reposados are rested for up to six months in ex-bourbon barrels.

NOM
1107

Region
Ciénega

Distillery
Tequila el Viejito, Atotonilco el Alto, Jalisco

Category
100% Blue Agave Tequila

Hydrolysis
Horno

Extraction
Roller Mill

Still Type
Hybrid Still

Brand Owner
Tequila el Viejito

Plata 42

Strength
42% ABV

Price
$

FLAVOR This tequila offers lovely aromas of cooked agave, dry mango, papaya, citrus, and damp grass. On the palate, it is velvety smooth with flavors of cooked agave, baked yam, and black pepper. The finish is long and semidry, with persistent notes of cooked agave and pepper, making it a clear, rich, and classically styled tequila that has returned after a long absence.

Reposado

Strength
40% ABV

Price
$$

FLAVOR This tequila offers a lovely aroma that is savory and fruity with notes of ripe plum, green agave, white pepper, and orange zest. On the palate, it's lean and fruit-forward with flavors of papaya, cooked agave, and oak, evolving to dark chocolate, black pepper, and dried mango. This is a fun, well-balanced, and classic reposado that is easy to recommend at this price.

Espolòn

NOM
1440

Region
Los Altos Sur

Distillery
Destiladora San Nicolas, San Ignacio Cerro Gordo, Jalisco

Category
100% Blue Agave Tequila

Hydrolysis
Low Pressure Autoclave

Extraction
Roller Mill

Still Type
Column and Pot Still

Brand Owner
Campari Group

In 1998, master distiller Cirilo Oropeza and Raul Plascencia (owners of Corazón, *see* p. 94) created Espolòn Tequila. Plascencia provided the funding and Oropeza used his more than 30 years of distilling experience to oversee the construction of Destiladora San Nicolas, and the creation of the tequila's profile. Oropeza wanted to create an exceptional tequila that was accessible for everyone. To do that, he made Espolòn from a blend of pot- and column-distilled tequilas. The aged expressions are proofed to 42% ABV and rested in American oak barrels with a number two char, which means the inside of the barrel was burned for about 30 seconds. Combining the incredibly low barrel entry proof and char level allows the tequila to absorb more of the sweeter, water-soluble wood sugars and flavors from the barrel, and less of the alcohol soluble and bitter wood tannins. Oropeza's tequilas found great success and, after years of growth, Campari Group purchased the distiller and the brand in 2008 for $27.5 million. At the time, Espolòn, which translates as "spur," featured an illustration of cock fighting on its label. But, a couple years after Campari purchased the brand, this imagery was swapped for the current designs inspired by the famous Mexican illustrator José Guadalupe Posada. In 2022, Espolòn released its cristalino which, according to the brand, was the last project that master distiller Oropeza worked on before his death in 2020.

Blanco

Strength
40% ABV

Price
$

FLAVOR This tequila offers soft, sweet notes of lime, green agave, kiwi, and white pepper on the nose. The palate presents bitter lime zest, cooked agave, pepper, nectarine, and grass, with a long, semidry finish. It's a versatile, citrusy, and grassy blanco tequila, perfect for cocktails or on the rocks. A solid workhorse blanco, it makes a great house tequila that isn't too expensive.

Reposado

Strength
40% ABV

Price
$

FLAVOR This tequila has a bright aroma with green vegetal notes, lime, and a hint of oak, developing deeper aromas of cooked agave, vanilla, and white pepper. On the palate, it's soft and smooth with green agave and citrus flavors, building to notes of oak, pepper, cooked agave, and a lively minerality. Overall, a solid reposado that is well-balanced between agave and oak.

Añejo

Strength
40% ABV

Price
$$

FLAVOR This tequila has light aromas of oak and unripe plum, with a faint cooked yam note. On the palate, it's bright and fun, offering vanilla, oak, lemon zest, and pepper, with increasing sweetness and acidity. There is also a vegetal character, like waxy lemon leaves, combined with tart strawberries and agave fibers. Overall, a standard oak-forward añejo with decent balance between the wood and fruit.

Cristalino Añejo

Strength
40% ABV

Price
$$$

FLAVOR This tequila has light aromas of milk chocolate, orange zest, and oak, with subtle earthy notes. On the palate, it offers sweet chocolate and coconut flavors that evolve into a dry, vegetal finish with lime zest and birchwood. The medium-long, dry finish features lingering notes of key lime, milk chocolate, and oak, making it a sweet and chocolaty añejo that's best enjoyed on the rocks or in cocktails.

Tequila Fortaleza is the brainchild of Guillermo Erickson Sauza, the great-great grandson of Cenobio Sauza (*see* pp. 158 and 167). It is made at Destilería La Fortaleza (which means the strength), built by Francisco Javier Sauza sometime after 1946. Javier selected the highest point in Tequila for the site, so he could look down on his competition. But inefficiencies closed the distillery after about 20 years, as production could not keep up with demand. Eight years later, in 1976, Javier sold Sauza and its new distillery but kept La Fortaleza.

After two decades, Erickson began to refurbish the distillery before launching Tequila Fortaleza in 2005. Fortaleza is made using many techniques that Cenobio Sauza would have used in the 1870s, including brick ovens, a tahona, wooden fermentation vats, and copper pot stills. Its blancos are proofed with spring water, while its aged tequilas rest in STR barrels (*see* p. 86) for six months for the reposado and two years for the añejo.

Fortaleza

NOM
1493

Region
Los Valles

Distillery
Destilería La Fortaleza, Tequila, Jalisco

Category
100% Blue Agave Tequila

Hydrolysis
Horno

Extraction
Tahona

Still Type
Copper Pot Still

Brand Owner
Tequila Los Abuelos

Blanco

Strength
40% ABV

Price
$$$

FLAVOR This tequila has aromas of wet stone, mango, strawberry, cooked agave, pepper, and cut grass. It offers a soft, peppery plate with sweet fruit and vegetal agave flavors, balancing earthiness, and fruity sweetness. The finish is long and dry with mango and cooked agave notes, making it an excellent, and complex tequila that reveals more the longer you spend with it.

Reposado

Strength
40% ABV

Price
$$$$

FLAVOR This tequila has a rich aroma of caramel, vanilla, and bright tropical fruits, reminiscent of a fun high-ester rum that evolves into melon and nectarine on a bed of oak. On the palate, the fruit and woody flavors continue, balanced by an earthy note on the finish. It is a delicious, powerful tequila that is a real treat to drink if you like fruit forward reposados.

In 2013, Enrique Fonseca and Jake Lustig collaborated to create Fuenteseca as a platform to bottle some of Fonseca's most unique and special tequilas. Fonseca is a fourth-generation agave grower, and all of his decisions around cooking, fermentation, distilling, and aging are based on how best to express the character of the agaves that has developed for almost a decade in the highlands of Jalisco.

Cosecha, which translates as harvest, is a limited-edition blanco tequila that highlights the unique character of agaves grown in a specific field or estate. In 2018, Fonseca harvested a special plot of overripe agaves grown at over 5,000ft (1,524m) in the chalky soil outside Vista Hermosa, Michoacán. After distillation, the blanco was held in stainless steel tanks for two years to allow it to rest and slowly evolve to fully express the terroir of this unique tequila. In 2023, the ADI International Spirits Competition named Cosecha 2018 Blanco Tequila the Best Tequila of the Year.

The aged expressions are proof that Enrique Fonseca is not just a master distiller but the greatest living master of long-aged tequilas. Most of the expressions released through this brand are extra añejo tequilas made from a single harvest that begin at five years old and extend to twenty-one years old, making these tequilas some of the oldest ever made. Most other tequila brands make their extra añejos using the same fermentation, stills, and barrels as their other tequilas but they age them for longer. For Fuentaseca tequilas, Fonseca tailors every step of his process based on what the agaves need to become the greatest spirit possible. For the 2015 harvest, 65% of the agaves were pot-distilled and then aged in used sherry butts made from French oak that previously held Highland Scotch whisky. The remaining 35% was column-distilled and aged in European wine barrels made from Quercus robur, a specific variety of oak. After aging for five years, these tequilas are married together and bottled at 41.3% ABV.

Fuenteseca

NOM
1146

Region
Los Valles

Distillery
La Tequileña, Tequila, Jalisco

Category
100% Blue Agave Tequila

Hydrolysis
Low Pressure Autoclave

Extraction
Screw and Roller Mill

Still Type
Column and Pot Still

Brand Owner
Tequileña

Cosecha 2018 Blanco

Strength
44.8% ABV

Price
$$$$

FLAVOR The aroma is captivating with notes of baked apples and pears sprinkled with cinnamon and brown sugar. On the palate, the tequila is dry but the sweet aromas carry over onto the tongue with warm flavors of stewed fruit and baking spices that linger for a long time. The amazing thing about this tequila is that these flavors come entirely from the combination of fully mature blue agave and fermentation by NOM 1146's house yeast. If you have never had a tequila like this, these flavors can be surprising and perhaps off-putting. But, if you give them a chance and open yourself to the flavors created during fermentation, then you are in for a great treat. With the amount of time and effort that went into the making of this tequila, the reverent choice is to savor this neat or with a small splash of water to tame a bit of its heat

Reserva 5 Years Extra Añejo

Strength
41.3% ABV

Price
$$$$$

FLAVOR On the nose, this tequila is light and delicate with aromas of elderflower, lemon zest, green mango, and cooked agave. On the palate, the spirit has a light sweetness and is slightly sharp with flavors of cooked agave, vanilla, and baked yam with a sprinkling of black pepper for added depth. The second sip reveals flavors of ripe mango, overripe banana, and a hint of milk chocolate balanced against a subtle spiciness almost like cinnamon, grated nutmeg, and dried coconut that come from the oak. The finish is long and dry with subtle flavors of oak, vanilla, caramel, and cooked agave. For a five-year-old tequila, there is so much liveliness and vibrancy still left in the spirit while it also presents some of the telltale flavors of a well-matured spirit. This tequila also demonstrates the beauty that can be achieved by blending expertly aged pot- and column-still tequilas.

G4

NOM
1579

Region
Los Altos Sur

Distillery
Destilería El Pandillo, Jesús María, Jalisco

Category
100% Blue Agave Tequila

Hydrolysis
Horno

Extraction
Tahona

Still Type
Copper Pot Still

Brand Owner
Destileria El Pandillo

Felipe Camarena built Destilería El Pandillo in 2011, and created G4 as his flagship brand to honor the four generations of tequila producers in his family. This includes himself (third generation) and his sons Luis Felipe and Alan (fourth generation) who are working at the distillery and will carry on the Camarena legacy. The agaves used for G4 are harvested when they are super ripe at 30°Brix (30% potential fermentable sugars). They are then cooked in stone ovens for three days, crushed with Felipe's custom tahona made from an earth compactor he repurposed from a junkyard for heavy machinery. The juices collected from each batch of agaves are diluted with either well water, spring water, or rainwater and then fermented without fibers using the same yeast that Felipe's father and grandfather used to make their tequilas. After fermentation, each batch is then double-distilled in copper pots and proofed using the same water source (well, spring, or rain) as was used in the fermentation. Some of this tequila is bottled as blancos or aged separately in "very old" George Dickel Tennessee Whisky barrels. From 2011 to 2022, Destilería El Pandillo only used stainless steel fermenters and all the G4 tequilas were made from an equal split of rainwater tequila and spring water tequila. In 2022, G4 released its first tequila fermented in wooden tanks and with agave fibers, called Madera. It is also the only G4 line that's blended from tequilas made with deep well water, rain, and spring waters.

Blanco

Strength
40% ABV

Price
$$$

FLAVOR This tequila offers aromas of dry mango, cooked agave, and black pepper. The palate features a light sweetness with notes of mango, cooked agave, and lemon iced tea, that evolve to include green agave flavors. There is an incredible balance and harmony between the fruit and agave flavors, making it a joy to drink. A truly elegant tequila that any self-respecting fan needs to try.

High Proof Blanco

Strength
54% ABV

Price
$$$

FLAVOR The High Proof Blanco has a soft aroma of green agave, mango, apricot, and lemon. Its flavor initially offers young mango, lemon, white pepper, and green agave, evolving to a more vegetal, artichoke-like taste on the second sip. The long, semidry finish features strawberry jam, lime zest, and cut grass, making it a complex and excellent choice for those who enjoy greener, high-proof tequilas.

Reposado

Strength
40% ABV

Price
$$$

FLAVOR This tequila has bright, green aromas of cut grass, unripe nectarines, green grapes, and white pepper. On the palate, it explodes with flavors of lime zest, green agave, cut grass, plantains, toasted oak, and papaya, offering a delicious dry and savory experience. This is an amazing tequila and a fantastic reposado that fans of G4 or Felipe Camarena must try.

Extra Añejo

Strength
40% ABV

Price
$$$$$

FLAVOR This tequila presents an evolving aroma from lemon zest and cut grass to papaya and earthy vanilla with hints of raisin and plum. On the palate, it's light and juicy with sweet flavors of dates, fig, and oak, balanced by agave fibers, cooked yam, and lemon sorbet. This lovely and complex XA maintains its core agave character without hiding it under vanilla.

In 1857, tavern owner Lázaro Gallardo began producing and selling his own tequila at his bar and, the following year, he named the drink Centenario in anticipation of the approaching 20th century. In the 1920s, Luciano Gallardo, Lázaro's son, bottled the tequila in its now iconic art deco-style bottles. On first sight of Gran Centenario's bottles, it's easy to assume that the brand is replicating a vintage style but these designs, with some minor updates, are original to the 1920s when this style was brand new. By 1955, Casa Cuervo had purchased Centenario and the Gallardos's distillery Los Camichines. However, the tequila was only available in Mexico for the next 40 years. In 1985, Cuervo attempted to trademark the brand in the US but failed because there was a brandy already registered under the same name. Ten years later, the brand had changed its name to Gran Centenario and, in 1996, bottles began hitting shelves across the US. All the Gran Centenario tequilas are made from agaves grown in Los Altos and aged for some time, which is a callback to the Selección Suave process that Gallardo created, in which he would blend aged and unaged tequilas together.

Gran Centenario

NOM
1122

Region
Central

Distillery
Los Camichines, La Laja, Jalisco

Category
100% Blue Agave Tequila

Hydrolysis
Horno

Extraction
Roller Mill

Still Type
Copper Pot Still

Brand Owner
Casa Cuervo

Plata

Strength
40% ABV

Price
$

FLAVOR This blanco has a strong aroma of cooked agave and lemon, with hints of ripe plums and dry straw. The palate begins soft and then develops a slight edge that enhances the flavors of lemon, baked yam, white pepper, and wet stone. More than just a pretty bottle, this is a classic tequila to enjoy while spending time with friends and family.

Reposado

Strength
40% ABV

Price
$

FLAVOR This tequila offers light, sweet aromas of oak, vanilla, and caramel, with very subtle agave notes. On the palate, it has flavors of tart lime, dry oak, vanilla, and baked yams, evolving with more citrus, pepper, and birchwood on the next sip. Overall, a fairly straightforward reposado packaged in a lovely bottle and best enjoyed in simple drinks.

Cristalino Añejo

Strength
40% ABV

Price
$$$

FLAVOR This cristalino offers light aromas of key lime, vanilla, oak, and a slight berry sweetness. The palate features flavors of fresh berries, cooked agave, and vanilla, with a warm but pleasant alcohol sensation. The flavors disappear quickly with very little evidence of being finished in Calvados barrels. If you are looking for a dry, light bodied, and fruity tequila then you may enjoy this cristalino.

Leyenda Extra Añejo

Strength
40% ABV

Price
$$$$

FLAVOR This tequila has a light, fruity, and woody aroma with notes of blackberry, licorice, violets, baked yam, green apple, and oak. On the palate, cooked agave, lemon zest, vanilla, and caramel flavors are complemented by floral notes and sweet stone fruit and dried mango. Overall, a very lovely oak-forward tequila that resembles other Cuervo XAs and is different enough that it is worth trying as well.

The year 2022 saw Casa Cuervo collaborate with comedian and actor Kevin Hart to release Gran Coramino. The brand launched with its reposado cristalino and has since expanded to include an unfiltered reposado and an añejo. The cristalino is aged for two to four months in new medium-char Eastern European oak barrels and then finished in Cabernet Sauvignon wine barrels. The other reposado is aged in new medium-char American oak barrels and blended with extra añejo tequilas matured in brandy and muscatel barrels. Similarly, the añejo is aged in new medium-char American oak and it is also blended with extra añejo tequila that was aged in ex-cognac barrels. According to the brand, it donates $1 from the sale of each bottle to the Coramino Fund, which pays out $10,000 grants to small business in the US, such as restaurants, cafés, personal trainers, and clothing designers.

Gran Coramino

NOM
1122

Region
Central

Distillery
Los Camichines, La Laja, Jalisco

Category
100% Blue Agave Tequila

Hydrolysis
Horno

Extraction
Roller Mill

Still Type
Copper Pot Still

Brand Owner
Casa Cuervo

Cristalino Reposado

Strength
40% ABV

Price
$$

FLAVOR This tequila has a light aroma of cooked agave, orange blossom, and earth, with a heavy dose of alcohol. On the palate, it's semisweet with orange zest and cooked agave flavors, followed by a stinging sensation and hints of vanilla and bitter oak. The long, dry finish features lemon zest, vanilla, and wood notes, making it better for mixing than drinking neat.

Añejo

Strength
40% ABV

Price
$$$$

FLAVOR This tequila offers aromas of vanilla, salted caramel, and clove layered with a touch of sweet pipe tobacco. On the palate, it's soft and sweet with flavors of vanilla, pipe tobacco, cloves, oak, honey, and orange blossoms. As sweeter style añejos go, this is very well executed and has a nice range of flavors that you don't get in other Cuervo añejos.

The history of Herradura begins in 1825 when Father José Feliciano de la Trinidad Escobado Romo completed construction of his new residence, Hacienda del Padre, where he raised cattle, and grew corn, beans, and agave. About 30 years later, Joséfa Salazar, the goddaughter of Romo, inherited the hacienda and hired Félix López to manage the farm and the distillery. When Salazar was no longer able to pay López to run the distillery, she decided to deed him the land instead. In 1870, López renamed the estate Hacienda San José del Refugio and began producing tequila commercially. By 1928, Aurelio López, Félix's son was running the hacienda and renamed the company and its tequila, Herradura, after a good luck horseshoe he allegedly found when walking around the hacienda one day. While other distillers eventually began making mixtos, Herradura has always made 100% agave tequilas with great pride. In 1994, Herradura released Selección Suprema, a four-year-old añejo that, at the time, was one of the oldest tequilas to be bottled. It set the stage for the CRT to create of the extra añejo category 11 years later. The family retained ownership of the company until 2007, when it sold it to Brown-Forman for $776 million.

Herradura

NOM
1119

Region
Los Valles

Distillery
Brown Forman Tequila México, Amatitán, Jalisco

Category
100% Blue Agave Tequila

Hydrolysis
Horno

Extraction
Roller Mill

Still Type
Stainless Steel Pot Still

Brand Owner
Brown-Forman

Reposado

Strength
40% ABV

Price
$$

FLAVOR This tequila offers aromas of cooked agave, lemon zest, white pepper, and hints of coconut and vegetal notes. On the palate, it features flavors of cooked agave, vanilla, oak, unripe plum, raspberries, and baked yam, balanced by a pleasant acidity. It's a nice reposado with balance and a slight sharpness to the alcohol, making it suitable for mixing or on drinking the rocks.

Añejo

Strength
40% ABV

Price
$$

FLAVOR This tequila offers aromas of buttery chardonnay, lemon, raisins, oak, and caramel. The palate evolves from oak and red grapes to vanilla and then again to sweet and sour lemon, unripe nectarine, and green agave. This is a decent oak-forward añejo albeit with a tannic bitterness.

Legend Añejo

Strength
40% ABV

Price
$$$$

FLAVOR This tequila opens with aromas of corn bread, baked yam, oak, maraschino cherry, flamed orange peel, and a nice spice character like a high rye bourbon. The palate is oak-dominated with flavors of wood spices, cherries, orange zest, and vanilla. The finish is long and dry with oak, orange peel, vanilla, and corn bread notes, making it a complex and enjoyable spirit for whiskey drinkers.

Selección Suprema Extra Añejo

Strength
40% ABV

Price
$$$$$

FLAVOR This tequila offers light aromas of green apple, peach, tangerine, and oak, with hints of cooked agave and vanilla. On the palate, expect flavors of agave, lime zest, oak, white pepper, and underripe peach, with a growing sweetness and a slight numbing sensation. There are light notes of mandarin, and yellow plums lightly drizzled with vanilla. Seleccion Suprema has a special place in my heart because it was the first extra añejo I ever tried and it drew me deeper into the world of tequila. While not perfect, it has a unique and bright fruit character that is absent from other extra-aged tequilas.

Don Francisco Javier Sauza created Hornitos on 16 September 1950. The name Hornitos translates as 'little ovens', a nod to how his grandfather, Don Cenobio Sauza, used to cook his agaves in brick ovens. For the first 57 years of Hornitos's existence, the tequila was only sold as a reposado. In 2006, they were purchased by Beam Global Spirits & Wine (now Suntory Global), who expanded the Hornitos line to include a plata (blanco) and an añejo.
A quality spirit and good marketing has propelled them into the top 10 bestselling tequilas for the last two decades. Today, Hornitos is one of few companies that does not remove the cogollo, the bitter stem that later forms the quiote, from their agaves before they are shredded. They say standard cooking processes (horno or autoclave) with high heat cause the cogollo to release bitter compounds. However, Sauza says that, because they extract the inulin in its raw form and use lower temperature hydrolysis to convert the inulin into fermentable sugars, it minimizes bitterness.

Hornitos

NOM
1102

Region
Los Valles

Distillery
Tequila Sauza, Tequila, Jalisco

Category
100% Blue Agave Tequila

Hydrolysis
Autoclave

Extraction
Diffuser

Still Type
Column Still

Brand Owner
Suntory Global Spirits

Plata

Strength
40% ABV

Price
$

FLAVOR The tequila has a warm and inviting aroma of fresh cinnamon, black pepper, and earth. On the palate, the tequila is bitter and semidry with flavors of cinnamon stick, lime oil, and lemon pith. The finish is long and bitter with sharp notes, similar to those you get when chewing on a lime peel. The Plata is enjoyed best in cocktails which take advantage of its bitter character, or as shots from the freezer.

In 2018, Maurice Tebele, his brother, Elliot, and their friend Martin Hoffstein, launched JAJA (the Spanish-language equivalent of "LOL") after touring Tequila. Seeing an opportunity to create a brand that "honors friendship, promotes laughter and celebrates tequila," they began with a blanco and reposado made at NOM 1137, followed by an añejo the next year. Through viral ad campaigns on social media, Elliot was confident they would reach their target market of young millennials looking to have a good time and who didn't want a tequila that took itself too seriously. JAJA received funding from the American DJ duo Alex Pall and Drew Taggart, also known as The Chainsmokers, and has been successful with its strategy, doubling annual sales in its first couple of years. In 2021, JAJA caught the attention of Proximo, the US-based arm of Casa Cuervo, and signed a global distribution agreement with the tequila giant. It also moved its production to the Los Camichines facility that is part of NOM 1102.

JAJA

Reposado

Strength
40% ABV

Price
$$

FLAVOR On the nose, there is a lightly sweet aroma like an oaky white wine. There are notes of vanilla, oak, pepper, and a light vegetal character from the agave. On the palate the spirit is bright and juicy with flavors of resinous pine, lemon zest, young oak, and raw agave. With the second sip, you'll notice a little more sweetness that is almost like lightly salted caramel and black pepper. The finish is medium-long and dry with lingering flavors of wood, lemon pith, vanilla, and pepper. Overall, this is a more wood-forward reposado that is still very youthful. If you enjoy clean spirits that are slightly sweet and taste of vanilla, then you will enjoy this.

NOM
1102

Region
Central

Distillery
Los Camichines, La Laja, Jalisco

Category
100% Blue Agave Tequila

Hydrolysis
Acid-Thermal Hydrolysis

Extraction
Diffuser

Still Type
Column Still

Brand Owner
JAJA Spirits

The Cuervo family has been making tequila for more than 250 years, though the brand Jose Cuervo wasn't created until 1900. Since at least the 1960s, Jose Cuervo has been a leader in marketing tequila, quickly capitalizing on changing trends and tastes. In 1953, Esquire magazine published the first printed recipe for the Margarita (*see* p. 176) and, as the popularity of the cocktail grew, Cuervo began an ad campaign encouraging people to use its tequila in the drink. In the early 1970s when the Tequila Sunrise (*see* p. 206) swept the nation, Cuervo published a recipe again. Then in 1977, the US Alcohol and Tobacco Tax and Trade Bureau approved Jose Cuervo Especial for sale in the United States for the first time. The transition from Jose Cuervo to Jose Cuervo Especial was virtually seamless and it became the most popular 51% agave mixto in the world. Cuervo spent decades building its reputation and producing a decent tequila but, subsequently, Cuervo Especial has become a bottom-shelf brand. Today, Especial is released in two expressions, a silver tequila which is unaged, and a gold tequila which is also unaged but has added caramel coloring to give it its golden hue.

Jose Cuervo

NOM
1122

Region
Los Valles

Distillery
La Rojeña, Tequila, Jalisco

Category
Mixto Tequila (believed to be 51% Agave)

Hydrolysis
Thermal Hydrolysis

Extraction
Diffuser

Still Type
Column Still

Brand Owner
Casa Cuervo

Especial Silver

Strength
40% ABV

Price
$

FLAVOR On the nose, this tequila's aroma is slightly fruity with aromas of bubblegum, decomposing fruit, and grape drink. There are funky notes, almost like shochu, which is made from rice and dead yeast leftover from sake production. On the palate, the flavors are very similar to the aroma. There are light fruit and floral notes that have this slight funk to them. The finish is short and dry with the same floral and fruity flavors that continue right to the end. If you approach this as a regular tequila, you will likely be disappointed. However, if you come at the aromas and flavors thinking of a mild baijiu—a colourless Chinese spirit—or a mild sake kasu shochu then there is plenty to enjoy. This is best enjoyed straight from the freezer or as a substitute in shochu cocktails.

Richard Betts and Joe Marchese founded Casa Komos Brands Group in 2017, with the goal of offering ultra luxury tequilas that better match the settings and occasions in which people are celebrating and drinking. They also wanted to help tequila break out of the US and Mexico, and become more common in Europe and other parts of the globe. Betts trained as a sommelier and, in 2006, launched Sombral Mezcal and Astral Tequila (*see* p. 74), both of which he later sold. Betts and Marchese decided to bring a bit of Mediterranean flair to the world of tequila and use some wine techniques to differentiate their spirits. Komos tequila begins with a base blanco, which is then aged in a variety of French oak, American oak, and ex-bourbon, red wine and white wine barrels, and sherry casks. They then draw on and blend these different barrels to create unique profiles for each expression. In the few short years that Komos has been on the market, it has been produced at three different distilleries. Komos production began at NOM 1137 before moving to NOM 1110. Today small amounts are still produced at NOM 1110 with the majority of production now at NOM 1607.

Komos

NOM
1607 and 1110

Region
Los Valles

Distillery
Tequila Orendain de Jalisco, Tequila, Jalisco

Category
100% Blue Agave Tequila

Hydrolysis
Horno

Extraction
Roller Mill

Still Type
Stainless Steel Pot Still

Brand Owner
Casa Komos Brands Group

Reposado Rosa

Strength
40% ABV

Price
$$$$

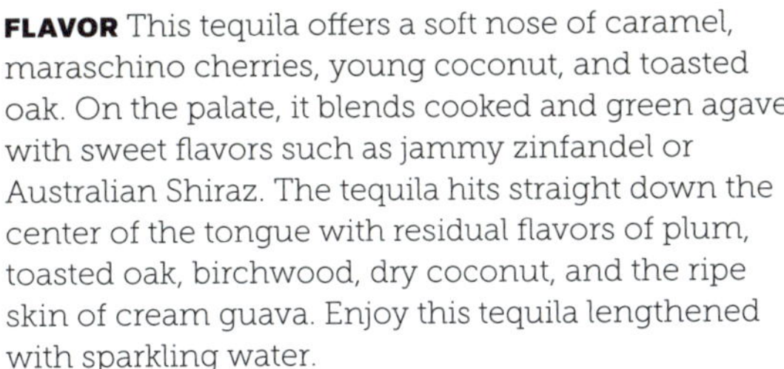

FLAVOR This tequila offers a soft nose of caramel, maraschino cherries, young coconut, and toasted oak. On the palate, it blends cooked and green agave with sweet flavors such as jammy zinfandel or Australian Shiraz. The tequila hits straight down the center of the tongue with residual flavors of plum, toasted oak, birchwood, dry coconut, and the ripe skin of cream guava. Enjoy this tequila lengthened with sparkling water.

Añejo Reserva

Strength
40% ABV

Price
$$$$

FLAVOR This tequila offers inviting aromas of orange zest, black pepper, vanilla, and salted caramel, evolving into baked yam notes. On the palate, it delivers a symphony of flavors including seasoned oak, vanilla, black pepper, and green agave, with subsequent sips revealing hard coffee candy notes. The finish is long with strong black pepper and salted caramel, fading into oak tannins and crème brûlée, making it a well-balanced añejo for those who enjoy confectionery flavors.

Añejo Cristalino

Strength
40% ABV

Price
$$$$

FLAVOR This cristalino has reserved aromas of lemon sorbet and birchwood. On the palate, it offers warm vanilla, caramel, strawberry, butterscotch, and coffee flavors. The finish is fruity with raspberry, strawberry, oak, and butterscotch. The underlying añejo is recognizable but the filtration process has turned the volume way down. If you like light, slightly tart, and sweet spirits then this tequila will be easy to enjoy.

Extra Añejo

Strength
40% ABV

Price
$$$$$

FLAVOR This XA offers a rich aroma of milk chocolate, caramel, oak, and floral notes like orange blossom. On the palate, it's bright and sweet with flavors of orange chocolate, lemon zest, and white pepper. This gentle, sweet, and rich extra añejo is enjoyable both neat or on the rocks, though it may not be as captivating as other spirits in its price range.

Around 2012, Andy Coronado, a Los Angeles-based punk guitar player, came up with the idea to create a tequila brand. After searching for the right partner, he decided to pair up with Melly Barajas Cárdenas, the owner and master distiller of Vinos y Licores Azteca. They developed La Gritona, which translates as "the screamer" and is a no-nonsense, classically made reposado. From the outside, the pared back packaging does a great job of sparking curiosity and encouraging drinkers to give it a try. Once in the glass, the tequila does all the talking—or screaming. After distillation, this traditional tequila is rested for about six months in used American whiskey barrels and then bottled at 40% ABV.

La Gritona

Reposado

Strength
40% ABV

Price
$$

FLAVOR The nose on this tequila reminds me of aged grappa with notes of grape skins and stems, vanilla, and light wood tannins. There is a very elegant floral character that is captivating. On the palate, there are notes of stone fruit, wet stone, pepper, and a light sweetness from the barrel. The finish is soft yet strong with lingering flavors of oak, green agave, and red grapes that end dry. La Gritona is a very nice tequila that is a little unusual. However, the flavors work well together and it is no surprise that it has captured so much attention. Enjoy this neat, on the rocks, or in a tequila variation of a pisco sour.

NOM
1533

Region
Los Altos Sur

Distillery
Vinos y Licores Azteca, Valle de Guadalupe, Jalisco

Category
100% Blue Agave Tequila

Hydrolysis
Horno

Extraction
Roller Mill

Still Type
Stainless Steel Pot Still

Brand Owner
Andy Coronado

Eduardo "Lalo" González Jr. and David Rodriguez Carballido founded LALO tequila in 2017 after the death of Eduardo's father, Eduardo "Lalo" González Sr. Both Gonzálezes were born into the tequila business, as the son and grandson of Don Julio González-Frausto Estrada (*see* p. 106). Lalo Sr and his brother created Don Julio tequila (*see* p. 106) in honor of their father's 60th birthday, so it seemed fitting for Eduardo and his friend David to immortalize Lalo Sr and name their tequila after him. The two friends originally created a special batch of blanco tequila to share with the guests at David's wedding and, according to them, everyone loved it so much that they decided to share it with the world. Their goal is to offer a Mexican-owned tequila that honors the agave and feels connected to modern Mexico. Because of this, they have committed to never aging their tequila and only selling a blanco and a high proof blanco.

LALO

NOM
1468

Region
Los Altos Sur

Distillery
Grupo Tequilero Mexico, Arandas, Jalisco

Category
100% Blue Agave Tequila

Hydrolysis
Horno

Extraction
Roller Mill

Still Type
Copper Pot Still

Brand Owner
Lalo Spirits

Blanco

Strength
40% ABV

Price
$$

FLAVOR The tequila has a lovely aroma of roasted agave, lemon blossom, and a light vegetal character. With the first sip the tequila bursts with flavors of dry mango, black pepper, and cooked agave. On the finish, the tequila lingers with notes of lime zest, and agave fibers that end with a pleasant mineral character. LALO has a great intensity of flavor and a traditional profile that can easily be enjoyed neat, with a splash of water, or on the rocks.

Lapis

Enrique Fonseca created Lapis Tequila as the crown jewel of tequila made from agaves grown in his hometown of Atotonilco el Alto. All the agaves used are grown at 5,200ft (1,585m) above sea level where they develop higher levels of sugars compared to those grown at lower elevations. Lapis—a semiprecious gemstone—has been prized among royalty for the last 6,000 years, so it seemed fitting to Fonseca to honor his hometown with a tequila named after it. Both the reposado and añejo are aged in used French oak barrels for a minimum of nine and eighteen months respectively to highlight and complement the underlying spice and fruit character of this tequila. According to records from the US Alcohol and Tobacco Tax and Trade Bureau, Lapis Tequila first entered the US market in the late 1990s. And, while it is not a household name, those who appreciate Fonseca's artistry tend to love what these tequilas have to offer.

NOM
1146

Region
Los Valles

Distillery
La Tequileña, Tequila, Jalisco

Category
100% Blue Agave Tequila

Hydrolysis
Low Pressure Autoclave

Extraction
Screw and Roller Mill

Still Type
Copper Pot Still

Brand Owner
Tequileña

Platinum

Strength
40% ABV

Price
$$$

FLAVOR This tequila offers aromas of green tropical fruits, cinnamon, lemon, dragon fruit, and green mango. On the palate, there is dry mango, cooked agave, and white pepper. This is a nice spirit if you enjoy blancos with notes of tropical fruits, cooked agave, and pepper. If the dryness comes across a little rough, try it on the rocks.

Reposado

Strength
40% ABV

Price
$$$

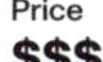

FLAVOR This reposado has light aromas of cut grass, wet stone, raspberries, apricots, and cooked agave. Its flavors are offering cooked agave, black pepper, oak, and chocolate caramel. The finish is long, semidry, with lingering chocolate caramel and a light oak dryness, making it suitable for those who enjoy sweet chocolate notes, on the rocks, or mixed with cola.

Maestro Dobel

In the early 2000s, Casa Cuervo's Juan Domingo Beckmann Legorreta (DoBeL) had a hunch that there was a group of non-tequila drinkers who would like the flavors that aged expressions offer, but that they did not buy or drink tequila because they preferred the look and perceived status of clear spirits. And so, in 2008, Beckmann decided to take a chance and create a new style of tequila that no one had ever seen before, known as cristalino. His new brand, Maestro Dobel, launched with the release of Dobel Diamante Cristalino, a tequila blended from reposado, añejo, and extra añejo tequilas that were charcoal filtered to remove the barrel color. As it turns out, Beckmann was right. Almost two decades on, cristalino tequilas have become the most popular tequila style in Mexico and one of the fastest growing styles of tequila in the US. Since then, Maestro Dobel has continued to push boundaries. In 2016, it made the world's first mesquite-smoked tequila and, in 2021, it produced the first pechuga-style tequila distilled with fruits, spices, and turkey breast.

NOM
1122

Region
Central

Distillery
La Rojeña, Tequila, Jalisco

Category
100% Blue Agave Tequila

Hydrolysis
Horno

Extraction
Roller Mill

Still Type
Copper Pot Still

Brand Owner
Casa Cuervo

Blanco

Strength
40% ABV

Price
$$

FLAVOR This blanco offers a strong aroma of cooked agave and a savory note that transitions to ripe apricots and peach skins, with a growing vegetal character. The palate presents cooked agave, ripe fruit, pepper spice, lime zest, and vegetal notes that balance its sweetness. This is a complex though somewhat rustic blanco that works nicely in almost any tequila cocktail.

Humito Smoked Silver

Strength **40% ABV** | Price **$$**

FLAVOR This spirit offers aromas of green agave, lemon, saline, and smoke. The palate features agave, smoke, lime zest, pepper, and dried apricot, with a long, dry finish that fades from grassy to smoky. If you are intimidated by mezcal, this is a good alternative. I'd suggest sipping this neat from a small glass with orange slices and a sprinkle of sal de gusano or Tajín seasoning.

Pavito Blanco

Strength **40% ABV** | Price **$$$**

FLAVOR This tequila offers a captivating aroma and palate of spiced oranges and ginger, with a savory umami note that likely comes from the turkey. It is difficult to pick out the agave, but the flavors are intense and a treat to drink in small amounts or in a cocktail. Best tried at a bar first, as a whole bottle may be too much.

Diamante Cristalino Reposado

Strength **40% ABV** | Price **$$**

FLAVOR This tequila offers aromas of vanilla, oak, and earthy spice, evolving into cooked agave and lime. Its palate is sweet and warm with milk chocolate, lime, vanilla, and caramel, gaining cooked agave and pepper with subsequent sips. Diamante stands out as a leading cristalino that retains its tequila character. It is ideal for those who enjoy reposados with cooked agave and sweet barrel flavors.

Reposado

Strength
40% ABV

Price
$$

FLAVOR This reposado offers warm oak, vanilla, cooked agave, and black pepper aromas, with hints of green apple and apricot. The initial taste is notably sour with tart lemon, green agave, and pepper, becoming slightly fruity on subsequent sips. While the finish is brief with oak, vanilla, and birchwood, the pronounced sourness makes it best suited for mixing with sweet sodas.

Añejo

Strength
40% ABV

Price
$$

FLAVOR This tequila has an earthy aroma with hints of vanilla and baked yams, evolving to a weak black tea and lemon. On the palate, it's spicy and sweet with oak, cooked yams, and a touch of candied mint, intensifying with cinnamon and clove. The long, dry finish is dominated by oak and wood spices, making it a passable oak-forward tequila.

50 Cristalino Extra Añejo

Strength
40% ABV

Price
$$$$

FLAVOR This tequila offers aromas of lemon zest, ethanol, oak, and spices, like clove and cinnamon. On the palate, it's semisweet and slightly sharp with flavors of vanilla, coconut, oak, dried fruit, and a hint of chocolate. The long, dry finish features lingering notes of raisins and dark chocolate. This is one of the better cristalinos in the Cuervo lineup, with hallmarks of an XA that has been subtly softened.

Mayenda

NOM
1440

Region
Los Altos Sur

Distillery
Campari Mexico, San Ignacio Cerro Gordo, Jalisco

Category
100% Blue Agave Tequila

Hydrolysis
High Pressure Autoclave

Extraction
Roller Mill

Still Type
Copper Pot Still

Brand Owner
Campari Group

Campari created Mayenda Tequila in 2023 as a new premium tequila celebrating the agave and named after the Aztec goddess of agave, Mayahuel (*see* p. 12). Campari has added two unique steps to the production process of Mayenda which aim to ensure the flavors and aromas of cooked agave are not lost during the distillation process. Overseen by tequila maestro Jesús Susunaga Acosta, the process begins by cooking the agave in stone ovens, milling, fermenting, and distilling once in a pot still. After the first distillation, the low wines, also known as ordinaro in the world of tequila, are then macerated with freshly cooked agaves to extract their flavors into the spirit. The agaves are then sent to the mill and fermented while the spirit is blended with the aguamiel (honey water), which is the free flowing sugary liquid that comes out of the agaves during the cooking process. Once blended, this liquid is put back into the pot still for a second time, which Mayenda believes produces a more robust flavor.

Blanco

Strength
40% ABV

Price
$$$

FLAVOR This tequila presents aromas of wet stone, cooked agave, and sweet plums. The palate starts sharp with lemon zest and pepper, then evolves into tobacco and an explosion of sweet baked apple and cinnamon flavors. This blanco is a real rollercoaster. It may seem a bit sedate at first but, by the third sip, the flavors get loud and you have a great time.

Reposado Double Cask

Strength
40% ABV

Price
$$$

FLAVOR This tequila offers distinct aromas of dry oak, wet stones, ripe plums, and black pepper. It features a concert of oak flavors, including sweet vanilla, caramel, cedar, pepper, and dry mango, with a silky smooth texture evolving into dry fruit, honey, and barrel spice. Enjoy this wood forward repo in a brandy snifter to allow your hand to warm the spirit.

Mijenta

NOM
1499

Region
Los Altos Sur

Distillery
Casa Tequilera de Arandas, Arandas, Jalisco

Category
100% Blue Agave Tequila

Hydrolysis
Low Pressure Autoclave

Extraction
Roller Mill

Still Type
Copper Pot Still

Brand Owner
Altos Planos

In August 2020, Mike Dolan—the former CEO of Bacardi—Juan Coroado, Elise Som, and master distiller Ana Maria Romero launched Mijenta Blanco as a new tequila focused on "community and sustainability." The brand's name is a play on Spanish term "mi gente," which translates as "my people" and references all those involved in the production of tequila, as well as the broader community of enthusiasts who enjoy the spirit. Four months after its launch, Mijenta released its reposado which is made from a blend of tequilas matured in American white oak, cherry wood, and acacia barrels. This is curious as the Norma (tequila regulations) specifies that tequila can only be aged in oak—though it's possible that the cherry and acacia barrels are used for finishing. Mijenta's añejo followed closely in 2022; it features tequilas aged in French oak barrels, which are then added to the three-barrel blend used for the reposado. As part of Mijenta's sustainability commitments, it uses carbon neutral packaging made from recycled glass and paper and became the first B-Corp certified tequila brand. This is a laudable achievement. Mijenta has also committed to allowing 10% of their agaves to flower, which provides a food source for the endangered Mexican long-nosed bat. This also has the potential to increase the genetic diversity of blue agaves, which is an important step, as most of agave plants are grown from clones (*see* pp. 27 and 36).

Blanco

Strength
40% ABV

Price
$$$

FLAVOR This tequila has aromas of green and cooked agave, mint, and oregano. On the palate, it's sweet with cooked agave, baked yam, and funky tropical fruit flavors, resembling a Jamaican rum. The finish is long and dry with lingering cooked agave and a hint of birchwood, making it an intense and polarizing tequila best enjoyed on the rocks or in cocktails.

Reposado

Strength
40% ABV

Price
$$$

FLAVOR This tequila offers aromas of milk chocolate and cooked agave. It starts sweet on the palate with notes of cooked agave, vanilla, caramel, milk chocolate, and dried dates, then becomes dry with grassy and sweet barrel flavors. This is more in the dessert-style though it is bone dry and the flavors are well integrated in the spirit.

Cristalino Reposado

Strength
40% ABV

Price
$$$

FLAVOR This tequila offers a light, fruity aroma with hints of mango, lemon, tarragon, and white pepper. The palate presents savory oak and dried herb flavors, balanced by sweet, cooked agave, lemon, and vanilla. This is a pleasant and savory reposado that is a nice departure from so many other cristalinos, which taste largely of vanilla extract.

Añejo Gran Reserva

Strength
40% ABV

Price
$$$$

FLAVOR This tequila has aromas of ripe berries, sweet wine, vanilla, oak, and a prominent fruit character. On the palate, it is dry with sweet flavors of blackberry and blueberry jam, layered with dry oak, cooked agave, and white pepper, which intensifies with subsequent sips. Overall, this is a lovely ripe, fruit-forward añejo you can sip neat or over one large ice cube.

Danny Schneeweiss and Moises Guindi created Leyenda del Milagro in 1997, with the goal of creating a tequila with an agave-forward profile that they believed was missing from the market. For the first couple of years Milagro was made at NOM 1173, but around 2000 production moved to NOM 1420. In 2006, William Grant & Sons purchased Milagro and, over the next four years, worked on building a dedicated distillery for the brand. Since then, Pedro Juarez has served as the master distiller for Milagro at NOM 1559. When it launched, Milagro followed a standard recipe of highland-grown agave cooked in brick ovens, milled, fermented, and distilled in both pot and column stills. After distillation, the aged expressions are rested in American oak while Milagro's select bottlings are made with tequilas aged in both French and American oak.

Milagro

NOM
1559

Region
Los Altos Sur

Distillery
Tequilera Milagro, Tepatitlán de Morelos, Jalisco

Category
100% Blue Agave Tequila

Hydrolysis
Horno

Extraction
Roller Mill

Still Type
Column and Pot Still

Brand Owner
William Grant & Sons

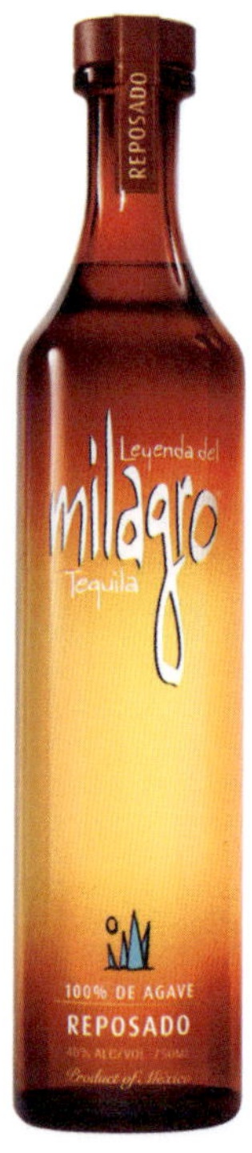

Silver

Strength
40% ABV

Price
$

FLAVOR This tequila has a bright aroma with notes of fresh agave, white pepper, and fresh pineapple in the background. The palate offers a slight sweetness with flavors of cooked yam, black pepper, and earthy agave. It finishes with a slight gum-numbing, bitter lime, and sweet cooked agave. A classic blanco that can be enjoyed on the rocks or in cocktails.

Reposado

Strength
40% ABV

Price
$

FLAVOR The tequila has light aromas of earth, green agave, lime zest, and ethanol. On the palate, it delivers a strong pepper punch, lime zest, and notes of oak and cooked agave. The finish offers cooked agave and sweet oak flavors. This is a good reposado for cocktails or shots out of the freezer.

Añejo

Strength
40% ABV

Price
$$

FLAVOR This tequila has aromas of mango, leather, and oak, with flavors of oak, stone fruit, and a light sweetness on the palate. The finish is dry with notes of pepper, lime zest, and oak. This is a nice añejo with minimal intervention, and suitable for cocktails or sipping on the rocks.

Cristalino Añejo

Strength
40% ABV

Price
$$

FLAVOR This tequila has aromas of marshmallow, lime, oak, and pineapple. The palate is dry with flavors of oak, cooked agave, and vanilla. The finish is short and dry with notes of oak, sweet lime, and well water; it's a simple, refreshing cristalino best enjoyed straight from the freezer.

Ocho

NOM
1474

Region
Los Altos Sur

Distillery
Cía. Tequilera Los Alambiques, Arandas, Jalisco

Category
100% Blue Agave Tequila

Hydrolysis
Horno

Extraction
Roller Mill

Still Type
Copper Pot Still

Brand Owner
Heaven Hill

In 2008, Carlos Camarena (of the famous Camarena family) and Tomas Estes partnered to demonstrate that the growing conditions and location of agaves, also known as the terroir, have a significant impact on the resulting tequila. With about 50 estates spread throughout the highlands of Jalisco, the Camarena family has agaves growing at many different elevations in many different soil types and terrains. Each of these factors create unique flavor characteristics in the agave that, when processed correctly, are perceptible in the final spirit. As the grandson of Don Felipe Camarena, founder of La Alteña distillery (*see* p. 159), Carlos is a fifth-generation agave farmer. He also studied agriculture in college and brings a deep knowledge of farming agave into his tequila making.

Each year, Ocho releases two or more blancos from different estates, as well as aged expressions. This is because the brand only harvests agaves when the plants have reached at least eight years old—hence the brand name—when they are at peak ripeness. And, just like with wine, Ocho makes it possible to create vertical tastings with its tequilas. You can collect tequilas from the same estate across multiple vintages to taste how annual harvest conditions impact the flavor of the tequila. Since its inception, Ocho has earned many accolades: in 2024, the ADI International Spirits Competition named Ocho's Añejo Tequila the Best Tequila of the Year and the Best International Agave Spirit of the Year.

Plata

Strength
40% ABV

Price
$$

FLAVOR This tequila has enchanting aromas of ripe pineapple, pine, earth, papaya, and chalk. On the palate, it's silky and sweet, evolving into bright vegetal flavors, white pepper, and a strong mineral character, with a long, dry finish of lime and subtle vegetal notes. A fantastic blanco; it's no surprise that this tequila is prized by those who love traditional agave-forward tequilas.

Reposado

Strength
40% ABV

Price
$$

FLAVOR This tequila has a bright aroma with notes of green agave, orange, pepper, and earth. The palate is soft with flavors of crème brûlée, cooked agave, grass, orange zest, vanilla, and light oak. The finish is warm, medium-long, and sweet with vanilla, toffee, and oak notes. It's an outstanding reposado and if you're a fan of agave-forward tequilas aged with restraint, this is the one.

Añejo

Strength
40% ABV

Price
$$$

FLAVOR This añejo's aroma is densely packed notes of raisins, cooked agave, lime zest, under-ripe pineapple, cut grass, and white pepper. The palate is lightly sweet with a slight creamy character. There are flavors of raisin, lemon-lime, and young mango followed by oak and leather. This is a wonderful añejo with all the hallmarks of a mature spirit, but without being buried in oak.

Extra Añejo 2015 Loma Alta

Strength
40% ABV

Price
$$$$$

FLAVOR This tequila has a vibrant aroma of green agave, cut grass, and green mango, with hints of cooked agave, raspberries, vanilla, and oak. On the palate, it's semisweet with flavors of green agave, green apple, tomatillos, and sour kiwi. This is followed by a warmth from the spirit as well as whisps of oak, vanilla, sweet cherry, and chocolate caramels. Best for those who prefer XAs with very little barrel character.

In 1967 whisky distiller Seagram & Sons saw the rising popularity of tequila and decided to jump on the trend, building a new distillery in Jalisco and creating the brand Olmeca, named after the ancient Olmec people of southeastern Mexico. Like many of the tequila distilleries of that era, Olmeca produced a mixto and it soon became a popular brand. Following Seagram's collapse in 2001 however, Olmeca was purchased by Pernod Ricard and had lost its relevance in the market. Pernod looked for ways to revitalize it and, in 2009, tapped UK bartenders Dré Masso and Henry Besant to create an updated version from 100% agave with a flavor profile that bartenders could easily work with. With these goals in mind, Masso and Besant partnered with master distiller Jesús Hernández to create Olmeca Altos: a 100% agave tequila that was accessible and could stand out in a mixed drink. Olmeca Altos was available as a blanco and reposado until 2015 when the brand's line expanded to include an añejo.

Olmeca Altos

NOM
1111

Region
Los Altos Sur

Distillery
Pernod Ricard Mexico, Arandas, Jalisco

Category
100% Blue Agave Tequila

Hydrolysis
Horno

Extraction
Tahona and Roller Mill

Still Type
Copper Pot Still

Brand Owner
Pernod Ricard

Plata

Strength
40% ABV

Price
$

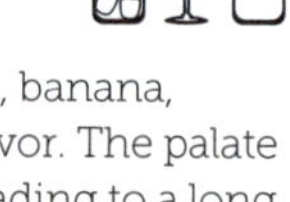

FLAVOR This tequila has aromas of lime, banana, and pineapple, with a savory vegetal flavor. The palate continues with fruit and spice notes, leading to a long, dry finish with lime, roasted chili, and cooked agave. This is a classic, highly recommended, and affordable blanco that is versatile for both mixing or sipping.

Reposado

Strength
40% ABV

Price
$

FLAVOR This tequila offers bright agave, lemon leaf, oak, and thyme aromas, with a mineral quality. Its flavor profile includes watermelon, honey, cooked agave, pepper, lime zest, oak, and vanilla, evolving with earthy and sweet notes. This agave-forward reposado is hard to beat when it comes to flavor, quality and price. An all-around workhorse of a tequila that can do anything you need.

Sofia Partida and J. Gary Shansby created Partida tequilas in 2004 from agaves grown on Partida's uncle Enrique's 5,000-acre (2,023-hectare) estate. Enrique was a third-generation agave farmer in the Tequila valley, outside the town of Amatitán. Partida and Shansby partnered with master distiller José Valdez to transform Enrique's agaves into tequila.

After distillation, the blanco is bottled unaged while the reposado, añejo, and XA are aged in used Jack Daniels barrels for 6, 18, and 48 months respectively. In 2016, the Edrington Group purchased a minority stake in Partida and took over distribution and marketing in the US. During Edrington's tenure, Partida released a line of luxury expressions called Roble Fino (fine oak). For these tequilas, Partida finished its reposado and añejo tequilas in used sherry-seasoned Scotch whisky barrels, which added additional layers of complexity. In 2022, Edrington sold their minority stake to the Dutch company Lucas Bols.

Partida

NOM
1502

Region
Los Valles

Distillery
Autentica Tequilera, Tequila, Jalisco

Category
100% Blue Agave Tequila

Hydrolysis
Low Pressure Autoclave

Extraction
Roller Mill

Still Type
Stainless Steel Pot Still

Brand Owner
Lucas Bols

Reserva Blanco

Strength
40% ABV

Price
$$

FLAVOR This tequila offers light aromas of green agave, blackberries, and citrus. The palate is earthy and vegetal with notes of green agave, white pepper, and lime juice. It has a dry, long, earthy finish. Overall, it's an elegant tequila that can be enjoyed on the rocks, with soda, or in cocktails.

Reserva Reposado

Strength
40% ABV

Price
$$

FLAVOR This tequila has aromas of vanilla, oak, and lemon blossom, reminiscent of its blanco counterpart. On the palate, it's semidry with flavors of vanilla, oak, green agave, white pepper, lime, and lemon. The finish is medium-long and dry, with a lingering bitterness from lemon zest and oak tannins, complemented by vegetal agave and a hint of vanilla. There is a delicate nature to the spirit that can be enjoyed in stirred cocktails.

In 2016, the Sanoma-based Sebastiani family created Pasote tequila in partnership with Felipe Camarena of NOM 1579 (*see* p. 73). When it launched, Pasote was made from a blend of 40% rainwater-made tequila and 60% spring water-made tequila. Pasote became a quick favorite among aficionados thanks to Felipe's involvement—and its reasonable pricing.

In 2022, Pasote moved to its current home at NOM 1584. Here, the highland agaves are still cooked in brick ovens but the juices are extracted with a mill rather than Felipe's hybrid tahona. The brand has also changed the yeast and it now uses 100% well water to make the spirit. Because of these changes, Pasote offers a unique flavor profile. Another development saw Maguey Spirits purchase Pasote in 2024. Maguey is a Mexican-owned company founded by Alejandro and Christian Rossbach and, since 2013, it has worked with artisan producers of sotol, mezcal, and now tequila.

Pasote

NOM
1584

Region
Los Altos Sur

Distillery
Tequila El Tepozan, San Julián, Jalisco

Category
100% Blue Agave Tequila

Hydrolysis
Horno

Extraction
Screw & Roller Mill

Still Type
Stainless Steel Pot Still

Brand Owner
Maguey Spirits

Blanco

Strength
40% ABV

Price
$$

FLAVOR The tequila has aromas of overripe fruit and chocolate, almost like chocolate-covered blueberries. It offers savory flavors of kasu and soy sauce on the palate, but without the saltiness, and then followed by chocolate and cooked agave. Pasote is a style almost unto itself and probably polarizing. Some cocktails may clash with its flavor profile so you will need to experiment and see what works.

Still Strength Blanco

Strength
55% ABV

Price
$$

FLAVOR This blanco offers strong aromas of overripe fruit, cooked agave, baked apple, and cinnamon. It has a fiery first sip with flavors of dried apricot, nectarine, cinnamon, nutmeg, lime zest, and cooked agave sweetness. Overall, a powerful tequila that can be used in cocktails in place of an overproof rum, and pairs nicely with ginger beer to make an El Diablo.

Reposado

Strength
40% ABV

Price
$$

FLAVOR This tequila has a strong, funky aroma with notes of sweet potato shochu, ripe fruit, koji rice, oak, and orange blossoms. The taste mirrors the aroma, featuring overripe mango, papaya, orange, cooked agave, oak tannins, and baking spices. It's a bold, funky, and lightly sweet tequila that may be divisive. Try it neat and warmed to get its full effect, or alternatively in a daiquiri.

Añejo

Strength
40% ABV

Price
$$

FLAVOR This tequila has aromas of green agave, cut grass, oak, baked yam, lemon, white pepper, raisins, and vanilla. On the palate, it's yeasty and earthy with pecan and Brazil nut flavors, transitioning to sweet, dried plums and cooked agave. This nuttiness is very unique and fun to drink. It also has great synergy in cocktails with other ingredients like orgeat syrup, maraschino, or even sherry.

Patrón

NOM
1492

Region
Ciénega

Distillery
Patrón Spirits Mexico, Atotonilco El Alto

Category
100% Blue Agave Tequila

Hydrolysis
Horno

Extraction
Tahona and Roller Mill

Still Type
Copper Pot Still

Brand Owner
Bacardi Limited

In 1989, the world of tequila changed forever: Martin Crowley and John Paul Jones DeJoria, of Paul Mitchell Hair Products, founded Patrón as a super-premium 100% agave tequila that they initially sourced from Siete Leguas (*see* p. 160). At that time, less than 2% of all tequila was made from 100% agave, there were no super premium blancos on the market, and almost none still used tahona. This sparked a wave of new premium brands, as well as super-premium blanco tequilas that hadn't really existed before. Patrón's emphasis on the quality of its 100% agave, tahona-made tequila also helped increase the popularity of the drink. In the next ten years, sales of 100% agave tequila grew almost fourfold.

By 2002, Patrón had moved production to its own distillery, NOM 1492. Thanks to its success, Patrón was purchased by Bacardi in 2018 for a reported $5.1 billion. It has become the third largest tequila brand in the world after Jose Cuervo and Don Julio (*see* pp. 106 and 132).

Blanco

Strength
40% ABV

Price
$$

FLAVOR This tequila has a bright citrus nose with notes of green agave and candied pineapple. The palate offers a light, sweet body with hints of lime and agave, while the finish is slightly bitter with lemon pith, earth, grass, and white pepper notes. While Patrón is no longer the cool kid on the block, it's still a solid, agave-forward tequila.

Reposado

Strength
40% ABV

Price
$$

FLAVOR The reposado has a light aroma of lemon oil, vanilla, and a sour-sweet hint of *pulque* (a milky alcoholic drink made by the fermentation of agave sap). Its palate offers a complex mix of oak, cooked agave, lemon zest, and vanilla, leading to a dry finish with notes of agave fiber and vanilla sweetness. This decent, lighter style is easy to drink and is a good introduction to more traditional tequilas.

Don Delfino González began making tequila for friends and family on his ranch, San Matias in Magdalena, Jalisco in 1886, and built a new distillery in the highlands of Jalisco in the 1940s. According to Pueblo Viejo's current CEO, González moved the distillery to Ojo de Agua de Latillas to be close to a natural spring that provided water year-round. The newly christened Casa San Matías continued to use the same tahona from the ranch but, as time passed, it, like many others, eventually upgraded to the more efficient roller mill. Over the next few decades, ownership of the distillery passed from Don Guillermo Castañeda to Don Jesús López Román in 1985. Four years later, Don Jesús created Pueblo Viejo as an authentic tequila at an affordable price. In 1997 Don Jesús passed away and his wife Carmen Villarreal stepped into the role as CEO. Master distiller Rocio Rodriguez makes the tequila today and, after distillation, the blanco is transported to the Pueblo Viejo Hacienda in Acatic, where it is bottled or aged in the cellars.

Pueblo Viejo

NOM
1103

Region
Los Altos Sur

Distillery
Tequila San Matías de Jalisco, Ojo de Agua de Latillas, Jalisco

Category
100% Blue Agave Tequila

Hydrolysis
Horno

Extraction
Roller Mill

Still Type
Stainless Steel Pot Still

Brand Owner
Casa San Matías

Blanco

Strength
40% ABV

Price
$

FLAVOR This tequila has a light floral aroma with notes of white flowers, honeydew melon, and papaya—almost like a sweet potato shochu. On the palate, it's clean and dry, offering black pepper, lime zest, and subtle pineapple sweetness. The finish is long and peppery, making it a great mixing spirit that will stand up in any classic tequila cocktail.

Reposado

Strength
40% ABV

Price
$

FLAVOR This tequila offers sweet aromas of vanilla, dried apricot, maraschino cherries, and fennel flowers. On the palate, it features flavors of oak, vanilla, white pepper, and earth. The finish is short and fruity with faint flavors of dark cherries and vanilla, followed by dry oak. This is another well-balanced option for traditional tequila cocktails.

Purasangre, which translates as "thoroughbred," is another great tequila created by Maestro Enrique Fonseca. According to records with the Alcohol and Tobacco Tax and Trade Bureau, Purasangre was first approved for sale in the US in 1997 when it was only sold as a reposado. Over the years, the line has expanded to include two blancos, an añejo, and an extra añejo. The defining character of Purasangre is that it's made from agaves grown at 5,200ft (1,585m) outside Fonseca's hometown of Atotonilco El Alto. After the agaves are cooked, milled, and fermented, the must is distilled first in a stainless-steel pot still and then a second time in a copper pot still. The aged expressions are exclusively matured in French oak barrels.

Purasangre

NOM
1146

Region
Los Valles

Distillery
La Tequileña, Tequila, Jalisco

Category
100% Blue Agave Tequila

Hydrolysis
Low Pressure Autoclave

Extraction
Screw and Roller Mill

Still Type
Stainless Steel and Copper Pot Still

Brand Owner
Tequileña

Blanco

Strength
40% ABV

Price
$$

FLAVOR This tequila has light aromas of cooked agave, dry mango, and lemon zest. The palate offers sweet treacle notes of burnt sugar, dry fig, and dry mango, with a long, semisweet finish of cooked agave, white pepper, and molasses. It's a delicious combination that's good for cocktails or neat, for those who prefer darker flavors.

Blanco Fuerte

Strength
43.5% ABV

Price
$$

FLAVOR This blanco offers sweet aromas of roasted pineapple, cooked agave, and dried mango, with some faint vegetal notes layered underneath. On the palate, it delivers pepper, cooked agave, baked apple, and sweet lemon. Despite its higher ABV, it provides a soft and pleasant drinking experience, ideal for those seeking a powerful blanco with cooked agave and ripe fruit flavors.

Reposado

Strength
40% ABV

Price
$$

FLAVOR With a light, tart, and fruity aroma, this tequila has notes of pomegranate, strawberries, and cherries. On the palate, tart fruit flavors combine with earthy notes of oak, baked yam, and cinnamon, with layers of butterscotch and vanilla in the background. Overall, this is a lovely reposado that has nice layers of sweet fruit, oak, and confectionery flavors.

Añejo

Strength
40% ABV

Price
$$$

FLAVOR This tequila offers a complex aroma of fruit, spices, and a hint of sulfur, alongside alcohol, agave, and oak. On the palate, it features oak, burnt sugar, cooked agave, and lighter notes of red apples, sulfured molasses, mango seed, and dry grass. This is a nice barrel-forward añejo though you may not enjoy this tequila if you are sensitive to sulfur.

Reserva 5 Year Extra Añejo

Strength
40% ABV

Price
$$$$

FLAVOR This tequila offers a dense, sweet aroma of baked yam, cooked agave, caramel toffee, and lemon zest. The flavor is sweet and spicy with notes of caramel, cooked agave, black pepper, and oak, alongside a funky mix of chocolate and tropical fruits. As you drink, flavors of sweet chocolate, coffee, overripe mango, and oak build on the tongue, making this a very fun and well-balanced XA.

Casa Cuervo first released Reserva de la Familia in 1995 as a three-year-old añejo, ten years before the Norma (tequila regulations) was updated to create the extra añejo category. According to Cuervo, this was the tequila the Cuervo family kept for themselves but eventually decided to release as a standalone brand. Unexpectedly, the launch of Reserva de la Familia coincided with Herradura's (*see* p. 128) and El Tesoro's (*see* p. 116) release of their own ultra-aged tequilas. Fast forward to 2020 and Cuervo has expanded the Reserva de la Familia line to include a blanco and reposado that are both certified organic. Reserva reposado is aged in medium-char new American oak barrels, light-toast new American oak barrels, and light-toast new French oak barrels for nine months across the three barrel types. In 2023, Cuervo added an añejo cristalino to the Reserva family. Made from organically grown agaves, the tequila is aged for a minimum of 14 months in medium-char new American oak and high-toast new French oak barrels and then finished for up to four months in Pedro Ximénez sherry casks. After finishing, the tequila is filtered to make it crystal clear.

Reserva de la Familia

NOM
1122

Region
Los Valles

Distillery
La Rojeña, Tequila, Jalisco

Category
100% Blue Agave Tequila

Hydrolysis
Horno

Extraction
Roller Mill

Still Type
Copper Pot Still

Brand Owner
Casa Cuervo

Platino

Strength
40% ABV

Price
$$$

FLAVOR The tequila has a lightly sweet aroma with notes of cotton candy, red apple, and wet stone. On the palate, it is soft with light flavors of lemon and unripe pineapple, and a hint of cooked agave and mild lemon candies that ends dry with a lingering metallic note. Overall, a light and quiet blanco that will be great for vodka drinkers.

Reposado

Strength
40% ABV

Price
$$$

FLAVOR This tequila offers aromas of vanilla, tropical fruit, cooked agave, and caramel with a hint of wood. It's a rollercoaster of flavors on the palate, which start sweet and soft, and then become sharp with notes of oak, vanilla, lemon, lime, and agave fibers. Overall, it's a very oak-forward reposado that shows decent contrast between sweet woody flavors and citrusy vegetal flavors from the agave.

Cristalino Añejo

Strength
40% ABV

Price
$$$$

FLAVOR This tequila offers bright fruity aromas of plum, raspberry, and blackberry, with underlying notes of ethanol and wet stone. On the palate, it's soft and velvety, featuring flavors of oak, nutmeg, sweet cinnamon, baked yam, vanilla bean, red apples, and banana. Overall, a well-balanced and decadent option for those who enjoy a dry añejo with flavors of dried and stone fruits.

Extra Añejo

Strength
40% ABV

Price
$$$$

FLAVOR This tequila has a light, woody, and slightly sharp aroma with notes of cooked agave, plum, and minerals. On the palate, it offers semisweet flavors of cooked agave, vanilla, candied orange, and chocolate almonds. This XA has a lot to offer and the combination of oak, fruit, and earthy agave make it an easy valley tequila for special occasions.

Sauza

NOM
1102

Region
Los Valles

Distillery
Tequila Sauza, Tequila, Jalisco

Category
Mixto Tequila (believed to be 51% agave)

Hydrolysis
Autoclave

Extraction
Diffuser

Still Type
Column Still

Brand Owner
Suntory Global

In 1858, a year after his father's death, a 16-year-old Cenobio Sauza moved to the town of Tequila and got a job at the Cuervo family's La Rojeña distillery. Over time, Sauza moved up in the business but, after a dozen years with the Cuervos, he struck out on his own and leased La Gallardeña distillery from Lázaro Gallardo (*see* p. 125) where he began making tequila on his own. By 1873, Sauza had earned enough money to purchase La Antigua Cruz distillery from Don Felix Lopez for about MX$5,000, which marked the beginning of his tequila empire. About 15 years later, Sauza renamed his distillery La Perseverancia which translates as "perseverance." Sauza was one of the first distillers to export his tequila to the United States and, in 1904, it won a medal at the 1904 World's Fair in St. Louis, Missouri.

Over the course of his life, Sauza owned 13 distilleries and planted more than two million agaves. When he died in 1909, his son Eladio Sauza took lead of the company where he stayed for the next three decades. Eladio significantly expanded the business in Mexico and saw the company through the Mexican Revolution and an agave shortage. Since 1974, the standard Sauza tequila has been a mixto made from 51% agave sugars and, in 2020, the brand name was updated to Sauza Hacienda. Both its silver and gold expressions are unaged, though the gold tequila gets its hue from caramel coloring.

Hacienda Silver

Strength
40% ABV

Price
$

FLAVOR The tequila opens with sweet and fruity aromas, almost like watermelon bubble gum. Underneath that are subtle notes of vanilla and fresh jasmine flowers. The first sip is semisweet and sharp with flavors of lemon oil, ethanol, unripe blackberries, and white pepper followed by a light earthiness. The finish is short and slightly bitter with more watermelon bubble gum, alcohol, and dry agave fibers. If you are a vodka drinker looking for an inexpensive tequila for shots out of the freezer, or for tequila sodas, this will do the job.

Similar to Jake Lustig's ArteNOM (*see* pp. 70–73), Siembra's tequilas are sourced from masters of their craft throughout tequila's denomination of origin. Restaurateur-turned-importer David Suro founded Siembra with the goal of bringing the highest level of transparency, traceability, and terroir into the world of tequila. Born in Guadalajara, Suro longed to find and share traditional tequilas with his restaurant guests in Philadelphia, Pennsylvania, and now the rest of the world. Siembra Azul, Siembra Valles, and Siembra Alteño offer multiple expressions from some of the best tequileros working in Jalisco. Siembra Alteño sources blanco, reposado, and añejo tequilas from Carlos Camarena at NOM 1139 (*see* p. 116). After cooking and milling, the must is fermented in wooden vats using wild yeast floating around the La Alteña distillery. It is then double distilled in copper pots, with the blanco proofed with spring water and bottled at 46% ABV.

Siembra Alteño

Blanco

Strength
46% ABV

Price
$$$

FLAVOR The aroma is bright and lively with notes of fresh cut lime, cooked agave, green mango, and pepper that blossoms into ripe fruit. On the palate, the tequila has a nice warmth with flavors of lime zest, pepper, and a sweet vegetal note that draws you back for a second sip. As you continue, there are sweet flavors of cooked agave while the pepper flavors build on the tongue. The finish is long and dry with flavors of agave fibers and lemon leaves followed by a hint of cooked agave before it disappears. This is a delicious and classic blanco that will be sure to captivate those who appreciate more vegetal and fruity tequilas. If it's a little too warm to drink neat, try adding a couple of drops of water.

NOM
1139

Region
Los Altos Sur

Distillery
La Alteña, Arandas, Jalisco

Category
100% Blue Agave Tequila

Hydrolysis
Horno

Extraction
Roller Mill

Still Type
Copper Pot Still

Brand Owner
Suro Imports

Siete Leguas

NOM
1120

Region
Ciénega

Distillery
Tequila Siete Leguas, Atotonilco el Alto, Jalisco

Category
100% Blue Agave Tequila

Hydrolysis
Horno

Extraction
Tahona and Roller Mill

Still Type
Copper Pot Still

Brand Owner
Casa Siete Leguas

In 1952, Don Ignacio Gonzalez Vargas created Siete Leguas ("seven leagues") tequila to honor Mexican revolutionary Pancho Villa's legendary horse. At this time, some distilleries were already on the path to modern efficiency. Don Ignacio however, focused on flavor and built his distillery, Fabrica el Centenario, with traditional brick hornos and a mule-driven tahona. After crushing, the pulp and juices are fermented with wild yeast in 10,000-l (2,640 US gallon) tanks and then double-distilled in copper pots. In 1984, demand had increased enough to build a second distillery, Fabrica La Vencedora. In 2022 the company expanded production with a third distillery, La Victoria. After distillation, its blanco is bottled unaged while its aged tequilas are rested from 8 months, 24 months, and 5 years respectively for reposado, añejo, and XA. Siete Leguas remains 100% family-owned and continues to produce its incredible, though somewhat underrated, tequilas that delight those in the know.

Blanco

Strength
40% ABV

Price
$$

FLAVOR This tequila has a bold aroma of cooked agave, fermented pineapple, and black pepper. The palate offers a sweet character with black pepper, lime zest, and candied papaya. This is a legendary tequila for good reason. If you enjoy other earthy tequilas, then this is a must-try. Enjoy it neat or in a more earthy margarita or paloma.

Añejo

Strength
40% ABV

Price
$$$

FLAVOR This tequila offers strong vegetal agave and unripe pineapple notes on the nose. The palate is big and expressive with cooked agave, green agave, and oak flavors, with a soft, warm alcohol finish and light note of white pepper. This is a wonderful agave-forward añejo and a good example of how tequila can be refined by time in the barrel, without overwhelming the soul of the agave.

As Lance Sokol traveled through Jalisco in the early 2010s, he met Pedro Hernandez Barba who had a tequila distillery and was looking for an American brand to partner with. Sokol returned to Boulder, Colorado, and shared Hernandez's story and tequila with his friend Laurence Spiewak. For six years, Sokol and Spiewak had talked about creating a tequila brand and it now seemed the time was right. After visiting the Hernadez family, they created Suerte—which means luck—in a partnership in which Hernandez would produce the tequila and Sokol and Spiewak would act as the importers and sell the tequila in the US. From the beginning, they knew they wanted to use a tahona to crush their cooked agaves so they commissioned a local stoneworker to chisel the tool from a 2-ton (1.8-tonne) granite stone. After cooking, the agaves are crushed and the juices fermented separately. The must is distilled first in a stainless-steel pot still, and then again in a copper pot still. After distillation the aged tequilas are rested in used American whiskey barrels while the blancos are allowed to rest for two months in stainless steel tanks before being bottled.

Suerte

Blanco

Strength
40% ABV

Price
$

FLAVOR This tequila is incredibly fragrant with aromas of lime zest, pineapple, cooked agave, pepper, and papaya. On the palate, it is soft with notes of white pepper, sweet orange, and cooked agave. While the body does not deliver as much flavor as the aroma suggests, this is a nice tequila with good agave character that can be enjoyed neat or in cocktails.

NOM
1530

Region
Ciénega

Distillery
Tequilera Simbolo, San Francisco de Asís, Jalisco

Category
100% Blue Agave Tequila

Hydrolysis
Horno

Extraction
Tahona

Still Type
Stainless Steel and Copper Pot Still

Brand Owner
Suerte Tequila

Still Strength Blanco

Strength
52% ABV

Price
$$$

FLAVOR This still-strength tequila offers aromas of cooked agave, wet stone, and fresh popcorn, with rich flavors of cooked agave, baked yam, and dark honey. The initial sharpness from the alcohol quickly fades, revealing sweet, cooked agave and black pepper spice. It has a long, dry finish with notes of lemon, dry grass, and birch wood. This tequila is ideal for those who enjoy rich and funky flavors.

Reposado

Strength
40% ABV

Price
$$

FLAVOR This tequila offers aromas of cooked agave, lemon zest, ripe pineapple, vanilla, and dry plum. On the palate, it features flavors of ripe mango, blackberries, cooked agave, oak, pepper, woody vanilla, green agave, and papaya. This is a nice reposado that leans into some of its sweeter flavors without being a sugar bomb. It's worth trying if you like fruit, cooked agave, and sweet barrel flavors.

Añejo

Strength
40% ABV

Price
$$

FLAVOR This tequila offers aromas of green plum, vanilla, light oak, and cut grass, with a bright palate of grass, lime, and green mango. As it develops, wood notes of plum, coconut, vanilla, and oak emerge, along with tobacco and cooked agave. It's a solid, balanced añejo with a long, semidry finish of sweet lemon, cooked agave, and dry grass. Enjoyable neat or over one large ice cube.

The Camarena family (*see* p. 79) has been growing agaves for more than five generations, so it is no surprise that they eventually started to make their own tequila too. Their first family distillery was destroyed during the Mexican Revolution but, many years later in 1937, Don Felipe Camarena founded La Alteña. Today, NOM 1139 is operated by Don Felipe's grandchildren: Lilianna, Gabriela, Jenny, and Carlos. The brand's flagship tequila is Tapatio, which is a nickname for someone or something from Guadalajara—their spirit has no connection to the hot sauce. For many years, Tapatio was only sold in Mexico, and so it developed a mythic status among aficionados. However, Tapatio can now be found throughout the US and the UK. Tapatio creates five expressions including two blancos; one reposado, which rests for eight months in ex-bourbon barrels; an añejo, which is aged for eighteen months; and its XA, which is first aged for five years in oak and then an additional ten years in glass jugs.

Tapatio

NOM
1139

Region
Los Altos Sur

Distillery
La Alteña, Arandas, Jalisco

Category
100% Blue Agave Tequila

Hydrolysis
Horno

Extraction
Tahona and Roller Mill

Still Type
Copper Pot Still

Brand Owner
Tequila Tapatio

Blanco

Strength
40% ABV

Price
$$

FLAVOR This tequila offers bright aromas of lemon and lime zest, followed by a sweet note of cooked agave, which is overtaken by cut grass and tropical fruits. The palate is soft with passionfruit, hibiscus, and agave, with an evolving complex of spice notes. This is a true classic, ideal for fans of agave-forward tequilas with a bit of fruit and citrus.

Blanco 110

Strength
55% ABV

Price
$$$

FLAVOR This tequila offers initial aromas of wet stone and ethanol, transitioning to lemon meringue and white pepper, with cooked agave and baked yam developing later. The palate is sweet with lemon and honey, evolving to include cooked agave, mango, dried apricots, and pepper. While it may be a bit rustic upfront, it gets funkier and more fun with each sip.

Reposado

Strength
40% ABV

Price
$$

FLAVOR This tequila offers bright, sweet, and fruity aromas of cooked agave, blueberries, lemon, white pepper, green grapes, and vanilla. On the palate, it delivers earthy flavors of agave fibers, dry grass, sweet orange, and light barrel notes with lemon zest and nutmeg. This is another classic tequila suitable for sipping neat or in cocktails like a traditional Tequila Sunrise (*see* p. 206).

Añejo

Strength
40% ABV

Price
$$$

FLAVOR This tequila offers fantastic aromas of cooked agave, lemon, pepper, and earthy notes, evolving to dried fruits. On the palate, it's bright and lightly sweet with flavors of lime, banana, cooked agave, white pepper, and a hint of oak and vanilla. This is a near-perfect añejo that all others are compared against. The agave and oak work together seamlessly to create a fantastic drinking experience at a price that cannot be beaten.

In March 2020, Dwayne "The Rock" Johnson, Jenna Fagnan, Ken Austin, and Dany Garcia co-founded Teremana Tequila and it quickly became one of the fastest growing tequila brands. Johnson partnered with the Lopez family, owners of Productos Finos de Agave in Jesús María, Jalisco, to create the tequila. The Lopezes anticipated the brand's success from the beginning, building a separate dedicated facility attached to NOM 1416 solely for the production of Teremana. While Productos Finos de Agave has every tequila making tool—including autoclaves, a diffuser, pot still, and column stills—Teremana is a classically made tequila with horno cooked agaves, that are milled, fermented, and then double-distilled in copper pot stills. When the brand launched amid a global pandemic in 2020, it began with a blanco and reposado. More than a year later, in December 2021, Teremana added its añejo to the line-up, which spends at least a year in used whiskey barrels before bottling.

Teremana

NOM
1613

Region
Los Altos Sur

Distillery
Destilería Teremana De Agave, Jesús María, Jalisco

Category
100% Blue Agave Tequila

Hydrolysis
Horno

Extraction
Roller Mill

Still Type
Copper Pot Still

Brand Owner
Siete Bucks Spirits

Blanco

Strength
40% ABV

Price
$

FLAVOR This blanco offers light aromas of lemon blossom, lemon curd, tart berries, crab apple, green agave, and white pepper. On the palate, it starts with bitter orange, dry lime zest, and cooked agave. The finish is long, semidry, with sweet, cooked agave and a light bitter citrus character, making it a decent blanco that's suitable for mixing.

Reposado

Strength
40% ABV

Price
$$

FLAVOR This tequila offers light aromas of lime, black pepper, and cooked agave. On the palate, it features flavors of grass, lime zest, lime pith, and a light sweetness from cooked agave. The finish is long, semidry, and earthy, with lingering agave and grass flavors, making it a good option for those who enjoy grassy and earthy reposados.

Tres Cuatro y Cinco is a special extra añejo created by Enrique Fonseca of NOM 1146 (*see* p. 71). This XA is all about the wood, and how blue agave can evolve and develop after multiple years in oak. To achieve his desired profile, Fonseca borrowed a technique from the wine world called coupage, where multiple unique elements are blended to create something new. In the case of Tres Cuatro y Cinco, it gets its name from its blend, which includes: 30% 3-year-old; 40% 4-year-old; and 30% 5-year-old tequilas. Each of these are aged separately in a sherry and California red wine casks made of French and American oak. This special tequila is bottled in handmade crystal bottles, with a sculpture of a biznaga—or giant barrel cactus—at the bottom of the bottle.

Tres Cuatro y Cinco

NOM
1146

Region
Los Valles

Distillery
La Tequileña, Tequila, Jalisco

Category
100% Blue Agave Tequila

Hydrolysis
Low Pressure Autoclave

Extraction
Screw and Roller Mill

Still Type
Copper Pot Still

Brand Owner
Tequileña

Extra Añejo

Strength
43.5% ABV

Price
$$$$$

FLAVOR Sweet and inviting on the nose, this tequila offers aromas of red grapes, raisins, and blackcurrants. This is followed by notes of oak and hints of cooked agave and cinnamon. On the palate, the tequila is bright with flavors of ripe strawberry and guava supported by an earthy oak note that quietly sits in the background. With the second sip, there is more sweetness and more spice flavors with baked yam, red apple, sweet cinnamon, and white pepper. The oak tannins slowly build on your tongue, providing balance with the sweeter flavors. The finish is long and dry with flavors of cooked agave, white pepper, and oak. Overall, this is a beautiful tequila. Its time in oak adds layers of sweetness and spice without hiding the underlying agave character. If you are a fan of Enrique Fonseca and want to taste something with a bit more fruitiness to it, this is a special tequila worth trying.

Tres Generaciones

In 1973, Don Francisco Javier Sauza created Tres Generaciones to celebrate the 100th anniversary of the Sauza legacy (including the 1873 creation of La Perseverancia distillery by Don Cenobio Sauza in 1873 and the promotion of tequila across Mexico by Don Eladio Sauza). The first bottling of Tres Generaciones was a specially aged añejo first released at the 100th anniversary party. Three years later, the Sauza company was sold to the Spanish brandy producer, Pedro Domecq. The following year in 1977, Tres Generaciones was released in the US as new premium tequila in addition to its classic Sauza and Hornitos tequilas. Over the years, ownership of Sauza and Tres Generaciones has bounced around but, since 2014, this storied company has been owned by Suntory Global Spirits. Today, both Sauza and Hornito tequilas are a shadow of their former selves but the triple-distilled Tres Generaciones tequilas still bring honor to the memory of Don Cenobio, Don Eladio, and Don Francisco.

NOM
1102

Region
Los Valles

Distillery
Tequila Sauza, Tequila, Jalisco

Category
100% Blue Agave Tequila

Hydrolysis
Acid-Thermal Hydrolysis

Extraction
Diffuser

Still Type
Column and Pot Still

Brand Owner
Suntory Global Spirits

Plata

Strength
40% ABV

Price
$$

FLAVOR The Sauza fingerprint is evident in this tequila, which offers aromas of cinnamon, baked yam skins, black pepper, and earth. On the palate, it is soft and bright with notes of lime zest, white pepper, and a touch of sweetness. The flavors are similar to Hornitos, though its execution is much better. Ideal for those who enjoy more earthy and dry blancos.

Reposado

Strength
40% ABV

Price
$$

FLAVOR This tres Generaciones reposado is a star. It has a light aroma of earthy agave, oak, and ripe papaya and it offers vanilla notes that complement the earthy white pepper and lime zest on the palate. The agave and oak are well balanced, making it an enjoyable tequila and a perfect choice for those who like earthy repos. Try it neat or in stirred cocktails.

Tromba

Eric Brass, Nick Reid, Jimmy Sherry, and Marco Cedano, former master distiller of Don Julio (*see* p. 106), co-founded Tequila Tromba in 2010. The tequila takes its name from the sound of the thunderous rainstorms that fall hard during Jalisco's rainy season from June to September. Sherry and Reid, who are both Australian, dreamed of bringing the high-quality tequila they enjoyed so much in Mexico back home. When they met Cedano, he had 40 years of tequila-making experience so they followed his lead in creating the profile and production process. Since then, Cedano's son Rodrigo has joined the company as apprentice distiller under his father. Tromba is made with classic methods of horno-cooked agaves that are milled to separate and ferment their juices, which are then double distilled in copper pots. The blanco is bottled unaged, while the other expressions are matured in American white oak barrels for just under 12 months for their reposados, 24 months for the añejo, and 36 for the XA. In 2023, Tromba released a special reposado to celebrate Cedano's 50 years in the tequila business. For this expression, the reposado goes through its initial aging period and is finished for an extra two months in French oak.

NOM
1547

Region
Ciénega

Distillery
Integradora San Agustin, Tototlan, Jalisco

Category
100% Blue Agave Tequila

Hydrolysis
Horno

Extraction
Roller Mill

Still Type
Copper Pot Still

Brand Owner
Tequila Tromba

Reposado

Strength
40% ABV

Price
$$

FLAVOR This tequila offers a fantastic aroma of green apples, cinnamon, honey, lemon, red grapes, and apricots, with soft oak and vanilla undertones. On the palate, it's smooth and sweet with flavors of apricot, vanilla, oak, baked yam, and honey syrup, followed by a peppery and bitter finish. This delicious, balanced reposado showcases Cedano's mastery and is excellent when enjoyed neat, with water, or in cocktails.

Cedano Reposado

Strength
40% ABV

Price
$$$$

FLAVOR This tequila offers a light aroma of dry grass, lemon zest, rose petals, and black pepper, with underlying cooked agave, lychee, and honeydew notes. On the palate, it is soft and round with sweet flavors of cooked agave, dark caramel, stewed plums with cinnamon, cut grass, and lemon zest. Overall, a very nice and well-balanced reposado that makes excellent use of French oak.

Añejo

Strength
40% ABV

Price
$$

FLAVOR This tequila offers a light and inviting aroma of oak, green agave, vanilla, and wet stones, evolving into dried fruit notes. On the palate, it presents soft oak and lemon flavors balanced with pepper, baked yam, earthy, and vegetal notes. This is a fantastic tequila that transports you to the highlands of Jalisco. It's incredibly affordable, especially for fans of vegetal and agave forward añejos.

XA Extra Añejo

Strength
40% ABV

Price
$$$$

FLAVOR This tequila offers a complex aroma of oak, minerally white wine, dried figs, dark chocolate, and caramel. On the palate, it's a balanced blend of sweet caramel, chocolate, roasted almonds, sweet orange, milk chocolate, and green agave with lingering tannins. A delicious XA that's worth trying for its elegant and enticing flavors, which are balanced between sweeter barrel flavors and agave.

Husband and wife Chad and Cristina Allen named their tequila Volans after the constellation, which represents a flying fish, and Chad's mother's Idaho-based fly-fishing lodge. Felipe Camarena (*see* pp. 71 and 123) made the spirit from a blend of his tequilas made using rain, spring, and well water. Unlike other brands, Volans launched with an extra añejo to sell primarily in Idaho and at the lodge, which has a largely whiskey-centric clientele. Near the end of 2019, Volans released its first blanco, followed by a reposado almost a year later, and a still-strength in 2022. By the time Volans got around to its still strength, Felipe had added wooden fermentation tanks at Destilería El Pandillo, which is why it is made from a blend of 54% tequila made with well water and fermented without agave fibers; 6% tequila made with well water fermented with fibers; 36% tequila made with spring water and fermented without fibers; and 4% tequila made with spring water fermented with fibers.

Volans

NOM
1579

Region
Los Altos Sur

Distillery
Destilería El Pandillo, Jesús María, Jalisco

Category
100% Blue Agave Tequila

Hydrolysis
Horno

Extraction
Tahona

Still Type
Copper Pot Still

Brand Owner
Volans Spirits

Blanco

Strength
40% ABV

Price
$$

FLAVOR This tequila has aromas of wet stone, mango, cooked agave, and lemon rind. It offers a soft palate with sweet agave, lime zest, and a long, dry finish that evolves into mint and cucumber. The tequila is reserved and nicely balanced between fruit and agave flavors, making it a treat to sip on a quiet day, no water or ice necessary.

Still Strength Blanco

Strength
53% ABV

Price
$$$

FLAVOR This still strength has a shy aroma of dried apricots and mesquite, with developing notes of black pepper and a savory, Pecorino-like quality. On the palate, it starts soft but becomes warm with funky flavors of overripe tropical fruits and toasted coconut that transition to dry vegetal notes. Overall, a really tasty spirit that is ideal for those who enjoy blancos with a bit of funkiness and heat.

In 2017, Moët Hennessy of champagne fame partnered with Santiago Cortina Gallardo to co-found Volcan de mi Tierra Tequila. Jalisco natives, the Gallardo family have owned Hacienda La Gavilana since 1774. The Gallardo's current distillery, Agrotequilera de Jalisco, was built around 2005 and, until 2017, produced tequilas for a couple of brands. However, once it signed with Moët Hennessy, NOM 1523 became a single-brand distillery for Volcan de mi Tierra. The Franco-Mexican brand launched with a blanco, reposado and añejo cristalino and, in 2022, it released its Volcan X.A. In the tequila world, the acronym X.A. has become common parlance for extra añejo, however Volcan's reference stands for Xtra Assemblage. This expression is made from a blend of reposado, añejo, and extra añejo tequilas so, according to the Normas (tequila regulations), it must be labeled as a reposado. Two years later, Volcan released its most recent expression: a blanco tequila made using a tahona.

Volcan de mi Tierra

Blanco

Strength
40% ABV

Price
$$

FLAVOR This tequila's aroma is captivating with notes of strawberry yogurt, cooked agave, and cut grass and, from the first sip, it is a rollercoaster of flavors. The spirit begins semisweet with flavors of fresh fruits and berries that, after swallowing, turns dry and acidic with lime zest, green apple skins, green agave, and grass. The finish is medium long and dry with lingering flavors of lime, unripe pineapple, candied orange peel, and baked yams. This is a very complex blanco that is packed full of flavors and is a real treat to drink. Each sip builds on the previous flavors, evolving with time. Sip neat to get the full experience. This tequila will also do an excellent job in a variety of tequila cocktails.

NOM
1523

Region
Los Valles

Distillery
Agrotequilera de Jalisco, Huaxtla, Jalisco

Category
100% Blue Agave Tequila

Hydrolysis
Horno and Autoclave

Extraction
Tahona and Roller Mill

Still Type
Copper Pot Still

Brand Owner
Moët Hennessy

THE COCKTAILS

Cocktails have played an important role in the rise of tequila's popularity. Despite the range of "classic" tequila cocktails being somewhat limited, tequila has proven itself to be very versatile and can easily work as a substitute in drinks originally built around gin, whiskey, and rum. What follows is a selection of 20 historic and modern tequila cocktails that showcase the spirit's utility—as well as proving there's a tequila tipple for every person, occasion, and mood. The cocktails range from rich and boozy, to bright and juicy, to light and refreshing. As you work through the recipes, you will find specific recommendations for blanco, reposado, or añejo tequilas; however these are solely recommendations. If you like your Ranch Water (*see* p. 210) with extra añejo tequila, or Margaritas (*see* p. 176) made with a cristalino, then by all means amend the recipes to suit your tastes. Spirits are to be enjoyed, so have fun and experiment.

20 Classic Tequila Cocktails

When building your home cocktail bar there are a few essentials that will make the process more enjoyable and help you to make better drinks. My first rule of thumb is to never skimp on the supporting ingredients. Fresh juices and a high-quality orange liqueur paired with a decent tequila will produce better results than an ultra-premium tequila mixed with bottom shelf triple sec and juices from concentrate. Now, it may sound easier to add a couple of measures of a top-shelf tequila to a pre-made margarita mix, but taking that little bit more effort to make your drink with fresh juices and quality mixers will yield a far superior drinking experience.

Here is a quick rundown on some key ingredients you will want to keep at hand. Many tequila drinks call for some sort of citrus juice, so having some lemons and limes available will allow you to make a couple of drinks when the mood hits. If you are having a cocktail party, you can juice your citrus the day before and store it in a glass bottle in the refrigerator. When juicing more than one type of citrus, write the name on a piece of masking tape and apply it to your bottle before filling it. This will prevent any condensation or spilled juice from preventing the tape to fully stick to the surface. Next you

will need a high-quality orange liqueur such as a triple sec, curaçao, or an orange-flavored brandy. All of these work well in tequila cocktails but personal preference on their flavor and level of sweetness will dictate which you choose.

Lastly is barware. You will need a few key pieces of equipment to make your drinks such as a citrus juicer, a jigger, and a cocktail shaker. As previously noted, fresh juice is key for making great cocktails so get a juicer that is easy for you to use with lemons, limes, and bonus points if it does oranges too. Making good cocktails requires the ingredients to be in the correct proportions to each other so the simplest way to achieve that is to use a jigger that has multiple measurements. In the US look for something that has markings every ¼oz up to 2fl oz, and for outside the US look for something that has markings every 5ml from 10ml up to 50ml. Next is the cocktail shaker. This can be two interlocking pieces (a Boston or Parisian shaker) with a separate strainer, or a three-piece Cobbler shaker with the vessel, strainer, and cap. In many cocktail bars you will see stirred drinks made in special mixing glasses. Those are nice to have but if you are on a budget or cupboard space is at a premium you can make do with mixing your stirred drinks in one half of your shaker instead of investing in a separate mixing glass.

With these few tips you can make great drinks at home. Practice makes perfect so if a drink doesn't turn out great the first time, try again and you may enjoy it more the next time.

Unit Conversions

1 dash
= ⅕ teaspoon
= 1ml

1 sugar cube
= ½ teaspoon sugar
= 2g sugar

1 bar spoon
= 1 teaspoon
= 5ml

½ tablespoon
= 15ml

Short Drinks

Short drinks are cocktails served over ice in a short glass, sometimes referred to as a rocks or an Old Fashioned. Larger versions are called a double rocks or double Old Fashioned.

The Margarita may not be the oldest tequila cocktail but it is the most iconic—which is why there are three separately named variations in this chapter. The earliest invention *claim* for the Margarita dates from 1938. However, in 1937, W.J. Tarling, President of the United Kingdom Bartenders' Guild, published a drink called the Picador with similar proportions in the *Café Royal Cocktail Book*. It's most likely that the Margarita and the Picador (*see* p. 190) were invented independently as a type of "Daisy" cocktail (spirit, orange liqueur, and citrus). Some stories claim that the Margarita was named after a woman, while others believe that the name derives simply from the Spanish translation of daisy. While the exact origin of the Margarita is shrouded in mystery, we know the first published recipe for the cocktail appeared in the December 1953 issue of *Esquire* magazine. Since then, it has become the single most popular cocktail in the United States.

Margarita

SERVES 1

2fl oz (60ml) blanco tequila

1fl oz (30ml) lime juice

1fl oz (30ml) orange liqueur

½fl oz (15ml) simple syrup

To garnish:

lime wedge, slice or wheel

coarse salt (for salt rim)

Combine all ingredients in a cocktail shaker with ice. Shake and strain into a rocks glass with fresh ice.

To salt your rim, rub cut lime on the lip of the empty glass. Cover the base of a small plate or bowl with coarse salt, invert the glass into the salt, lift, and gently tap to remove the loose salt.

VARIATIONS:

For a spicy margarita there are two easy methods. First method: muddle seeded slices of fresh jalapeño in the bottom of your cocktail shaker with your lime juice. You can control the heat level by the number of jalapeño slices you add. Add the remaining ingredients and shake with ice and double strain into a rocks glass with fresh ice.

Second method: add 1fl oz (30ml) of Ancho Reyes Chili Liqueur along with the original volumes of tequila and lime juice. Reduce your orange liqueur to ½fl oz (15ml) and simple syrup to ¼fl oz (7ml).

We do not know the origins of the Mexican Firing Squad cocktail. However, American author Charles H. Baker Jr. encountered the drink for the first time in 1937 at the La Cucaracha Bar in Mexico City and published the recipe in his 1939 book *The Gentleman's Companion*. According to Baker, he and his companions ditched their chaperones who were herding them into fancy and dull places that served warm drinks, and escaped to the La Cucaracha where they "almost became wrecked upon" this bright, tart, and refreshing drink.

Mexican Firing Squad

Combine all ingredients in a cocktail shaker with ice. Shake until cold, strain into a rocks glass with fresh ice and garnish with the lime wheel.

SERVES 1

2fl oz (60ml) blanco tequila

¾fl oz (22ml) lime juice

¾fl oz (22ml) grenadine

4 dashes Angostura bitters

To garnish:
lime wheel

Also known as a tequila Negroni, the Agavoni is another example of the incredibly flexible and adaptable combination of a spirit, Campari, and sweet vermouth. While it is likely this drink has existed for quite some time, its invention is first cited in Robert Hess' 2008 book *The Essential Bartender's Guide*. Hess credits German bartender Bastian Heuser for creating the drink for the Berlin-based *Mixology* magazine.

Agavoni

SERVES 1

1fl oz (30ml) blanco tequila

1fl oz (30ml) sweet vermouth

1fl oz (30ml) Campari

To garnish:
orange peel

Add all the ingredients into a mixing glass, fill with ice and stir for about 20 seconds. Strain the contents over a large cube of ice in a rocks glass. To garnish, twist a piece of orange peel over the glass to express the oils and then drop it into the drink.

VARIATIONS:
Depending on your preferences, you can use an aged tequila in this cocktail. If the drink tastes out of balance, try adding a bit more: 1¼fl oz (37ml) or 1½fl oz (45ml) tequila to 1fl oz (30ml) Campari and 1fl oz (30ml) sweet vermouth usually does the trick. For a more elegant presentation, serve the drink in a chilled coupe. If you do not have a mixing glass, you can build the drink in your rocks glass before serving.

Julio Bermejo created the Tommy's Margarita in the early 1990s at Tommy's Mexican Restaurant in San Francisco, California. Bermejo believed that 100% agave tequila was a world-class spirit that deserved respect and designed the cocktail to draw attention to it at a time when mixtos dominated sales in the US. This variation substitutes the Margarita's orange liqueur with a smaller amount of agave syrup which allows the tequila to take center stage.

Tommy's Margarita

Combine all ingredients in a cocktail shaker with ice. Shake until cold and strain into a rocks glass with fresh ice.

To salt your rim, rub cut lime on the lip of the empty glass. Cover the base of a small plate or bowl with coarse salt, invert the glass into the salt, lift, and gently tap to remove the loose salt.

SERVES 1

2fl oz (60ml) blanco tequila

1fl oz (30ml) lime juice, freshly squeezed

½fl oz (15ml) agave nectar

To garnish:
lime wedge, slice or wheel

coarse salt (for salt rim)

The Tequila Bee's Knees is a variation of the famous Prohibition-era gin cocktail of the same name. Simply swapping out the gin for tequila takes the drink in a new direction and works particularly well when paired with a more vegetal or citrus-forward spirit.

Tequila Bee's Knees

SERVES 1

For the honey syrup (makes 9fl oz/250ml)
4fl oz (125ml) honey

2fl oz (60ml) reposado tequila

1fl oz (30ml) honey syrup

¾fl oz (22ml) lemon juice

To garnish
lemon peel

To make the honey syrup, place equal parts honey along with 4fl oz (125ml) water in a saucepan over a medium heat. Gently heat and stir until the honey has fully dissolved. Allow to cool and transfer to a sterilized glass bottle. This will keep for a month.

To make the Bee's Knees, combine the tequila, honey syrup, and lemon juice in a cocktail shaker with ice. Shake until cold and strain into the chilled rocks glass with fresh ice. Garnish with a curl of lemon peel.

VARIATIONS:
If you are a fan of mezcal, try rinsing a chilled coupe or cocktail glass with a dash of the Mexican spirit. While it may not sound like much, a small amount of mezcal will add an aromatic complexity to the final drink. Prepare the rest of the cocktail as normal.

The Tequila Old Fashioned is a version of the "proto-cocktail formula" first recorded in 1806 as "spirits of any kind, sugar, water, and bitters." While an Old Fashioned is most often associated with whiskey, aged (añejo) tequila offers an excellent variation. The term Old Fashioned first appeared in print in 1880 and was used to differentiate it from the "Improved Cocktail" developed by famed barman, Jerry Thomas.

Tequila Old Fashioned

Combine all ingredients in a rock glass. Add a large ice cube and stir. Take a 2-in (5-cm) strip of orange peel and express the oils by twisting or pinching over the glass. Place the peel in the drink to finish.

VARIATIONS:
With such a simple recipe, the variations are endless. Simply changing the tequila, its age (añejo or extra añejo), the sweetener (agave syrup is a popular substitute for simple syrup), and the bitters will have dramatic effects. Try Mexican chocolate bitters for a chocolatey taste, or mole bitters for a bit of spice.

SERVES 1

2fl oz (60ml) añejo tequila

¼fl oz (7ml) simple syrup

1 dash Angostura bitters

To garnish:
orange peel

Drinks Served Up

This name refers to a set of cocktails which are mixed and strained into a chilled glass with a stem, usually a Martini glass or a coupe. Drinks served up are never poured into the glass over ice.

Albert Hernandez is credited for creating the original blended Margarita in 1947 at La Plaza Restaurant in La Jolla, California. According to some, the restaurant owner Moe Locke encountered the Margarita on one of his many trips across the border in Baja California, Mexico. Locke brought the recipe back but it was Hernandez who came up with the idea to blend the drink and salt the rim of the glass.

In 1971, entrepreneur Mariano Martinez opened a restaurant in Dallas where up to 200 Frozen Margaritas were served a night—all from one blender. Concerned with how to keep pace with demand while maintaining the quality of each drink, Martinez was inspired by a slushie machine he saw in a 7-Eleven convenience store. He bought a used soft-serve ice cream machine and adapted his family Margarita recipe, creating the first ever pre-made Frozen Margarita without a blender.

Frozen Margarita

SERVES 2

4fl oz (120ml) blanco tequila

2fl oz (60ml) lime juice

2fl oz (60ml) orange liqueur

1fl oz (30ml) simple syrup

24fl oz (720ml) ice

To garnish:

lime wedge, slice or wheel

coarse salt (for salt rim)

Add all the ingredients to your blender and blend until smooth, between 30 and 60 seconds.

To salt the rim of your glass, roll the lip of the chilled glass on a plate of coarse salt. If the glass is not pre-chilled, rub cut lime on the lip of the empty glass. Cover the base of a small plate or bowl with coarse salt, invert the glass into the salt, lift, and gently tap to remove the loose salt.

Pour the cocktail into two chilled, salt-rimmed Margarita glasses.

VARIATIONS:

If you do not have stemmed Margarita glasses, you can use a rocks glass. If you prefer a little spice in your margarita, one easy variation is to garnish the rim of your glass with Tajín—a ready-made mixture of dried chile peppers, crystalized lime juice, and sea salt.

First published by the Englishman William J. Tarling in the 1937 *Café Royal Cocktail Book*, the Picador is one of the oldest known tequila cocktails and predates the classic Margarita. The term "picador" refers to a Spanish horseman who assists in the country's bullfighting tradition. When it comes to the cocktail, however, a Picador is a spirit-forward drink that, like the Margarita, pairs tequila with orange liqueur and lime juice. Unlike the Margarita, the Picador does not call for simple syrup, so the finished drink is tarter and dryer than the more prolific of the pair.

Picador

SERVES 1

2fl oz (60ml) blanco tequila

1fl oz (30ml) orange liqueur

1fl oz (30ml) lime juice

Optional garnish:
lime twist

Combine all the ingredients in a cocktail shaker with ice. Shake until cold and strain into a chilled, stemmed cocktail glass. Garnish with a lime twist.

Katie Stipe, a bartender at New York's Flatiron Lounge, created the Siesta cocktail in 2006 as a variation on the Hemingway Daiquiri. Stipe decided to swap the white rum for a blanco tequila, and the traditional maraschino liqueur for Campari to make a more savory and tart drink. Stipe also recommends adding in a pinch of Kosher salt (coarse sea salt flakes) to amplify the flavors, and also as an homage to the Margarita.

Siesta

Combine all ingredients in a cocktail shaker with ice. Shake until cold and double strain into a chilled, stemmed cocktail glass. Garnish with a twist of grapefruit peel.

SERVES 1

1½fl oz (45ml) blanco tequila

½fl oz (15ml) grapefruit juice

¾fl oz (22ml) lime juice

¾fl oz (22ml) simple syrup

¼fl oz (7ml) Campari

pinch of kosher salt/sea salt flakes, optional

To garnish:
grapefruit peel

Also known as the Tequila Manhattan, Distrito Federal is named after Mexico City's alternative moniker. According to Avión Tequila, the drink was first created using the brand's spirit at an unnamed bar in Mexico City's popular Condesa neighborhood. However, Avión also credits Julio Bermejo as the creator of the cocktail at Tommy's Mexican Restaurant in the 1990s. Given Bermejo's leadership in helping popularize 100% agave tequila, it seems equally likely that he either encountered the drink in Mexico City and brought it back to San Francisco, or created it on his own as a Manhattan variation for the patrons at Tommy's.

Distrito Federal

SERVES 1

2fl oz (60ml) reposado tequila

1fl oz (30ml) sweet vermouth

2 dashes orange bitters

To garnish:
lime twist

cocktail cherry (optional)

Combine all ingredients in a mixing glass with ice. Stir until chilled, strain into a chilled cocktail glass and garnish with a lime twist and a cocktail cherry.

Jim Meehan, founder of New York's famed bar, Please Don't Tell, created the White Dragon as a variation on the classic gin cocktail, the White Lady. Meehan originally designed the drink around Casa Dragones' blanco tequila, but any high quality blanco will do the job, especially if it has a strong orange character.

White Dragon

Combine all ingredients in a cocktail shaker without ice and dry shake for about 15 seconds. Fill the shaker with ice and shake again until chilled. Double strain into a chilled coupe or stemmed cocktail glass. To garnish, twist or pinch the orange peel over the glass to express the oils then add to the drink.

SERVES 1

1¾fl oz (52ml) blanco tequila

¾fl oz (22ml) orange liqueur

¾fl oz (22ml) lemon juice

1 egg white

To garnish:
orange peel

The Corpse Reviver is a classic equal parts cocktail that comes from the late 19th century and calls for gin, blanc vermouth, orange liqueur, lemon juice, and a dash of absinthe. It was one of many cocktails designed as a pick-me-up to revive drinkers after a long evening of merriment. The drink was revived in the 1930s by Harry Craddock at The Savoy hotel's American Bar in London and has remained on the drinks menus of fine bars ever since. The cocktail's simplicity and balance make it easily adaptable and it has spawned innumerable variations—including this one, made with tequila.

Corpse Reviver Numero Dos

SERVES 1

¾fl oz (22ml) blanco tequila

¾fl oz (22ml) blanc or bianco vermouth

¾fl oz (22ml) orange liqueur

¾fl oz (22ml) lime juice

2 dashes absinthe

Combine all ingredients in a cocktail shaker with ice. Shake until chilled and double strain into a chilled coupe or stemmed cocktail glass.

Another cocktail that hails from W.J. Tarling's *Café Royal Cocktail Book* (*see* pp. 21, 176, and 190) is the Toreador. The original recipe calls for half tequila, and a quarter each of apricot liqueur and lime or lemon juice—which follows the same proportions of Tarling's Picador and Matador cocktails. Today, most Toreador recipes call for lime juice as well as a bar spoon or two of simple syrup to balance the intense acidity. Tia Zandona, co-owner of the drinks platform EZdrinking, found that if you split the citrus base between both lemon and lime, you don't need the additional sugar.

Toreador '25

Combine all ingredients in cocktail shaker with ice. Shake until cold and double strain into a chilled cocktail glass and garnish with a lime twist.

SERVES 1

2fl oz (60ml) blanco tequila

¾fl oz (22ml) apricot liqueur

½fl oz (15ml) lime juice

½fl oz (15ml) lemon juice

To garnish:
lime twist

Tall Drinks

As the name implies, tall drinks are cocktails served in tall glasses over ice with a good amount of soda, tonic, or another non-alcoholic mixer that lengthens the drink. Tall drinks are refreshing and less spirit forward.

One of the most popular tequila cocktails in Mexico, the Paloma is a tart and refreshing tall cocktail that combines tequila with grapefruit soda. One advantage of the drink's simplicity is it can easily be made—and remade—while entertaining. According to Camper English, a San Francisco-based cocktail and spirits writer, the earliest written reference of the Paloma as a named drink doesn't show up until the late 1990s. There are, however, advertisements by Squirt dating from 1950 where the grapefruit-flavored soft drink brand recommend mixing their soda with tequila, apple jack, or sloe gin. It is also interesting to note that Squirt was invented in Phoenix, Arizona, and wasn't exported to Mexico until 1955—meaning the "first" Paloma was probably made stateside.

Paloma

SERVES 1

2fl oz (60ml) blanco tequila

1 pinch kosher salt (coarse sea salt flakes)

half a lime

grapefruit soda, to top

Fill a highball glass with ice and add the tequila with a pinch of salt. Squeeze half a lime into the glass and top off with grapefruit soda.

VARIATIONS:
For a fresher variation, mix 2fl oz (60ml) of both tequila and grapefruit juice in a highball glass filled with ice, add ½fl oz (15ml) of lime juice and top off with soda water.

The Bloody Maria is a tequila variation of the classic Bloody Mary. According to Jack McGarry, co-founder of New York's The Dead Rabbit bar, the Bloody Mary was most likely invented in the US in the 1930s. However, the first reference to a Bloody *Maria* doesn't show up in print until July 1961, when a recipe called for rum rather than vodka. But, according to McGarry, this quickly changed to tequila, in part because of the popularity of a premade Bloody Mary mix. Companies that made these mixes were more interested in people buying their product and using any liquor they had rather than them sticking to vodka. But by 1972, the same year the Tequila Sunrise began to take off, tequila was firmly entrenched as the defining feature of the Bloody Maria. Tia Zandona of EZdrinking developed this recipe in 2013 for the South at SF Jazz bar in San Francisco.

Bloody Maria

Add the first six ingredients to a pint glass, squeeze in the juice from the lemon wedge, and drop into the glass. Add ice and stir. Add the tequila, top with Clamato juice, stir again, and garnish as desired.

VARIATIONS:
For a less daring take on the Bloody Maria, substitute the Clamato for tomato or another vegetable juice.

SERVES 1

1 bar spoon horseradish

1 bar spoon Worcestershire sauce

1 bar spoon Tabasco sauce

1 bar spoon of olive brine

1 pinch of salt and pepper

1 pinch of celery salt

1 lemon wedge

2fl oz (60ml) blanco tequila

Clamato juice, to top

garnish options
lime wedge, celery stalk, cucumber spear, pickled vegetables, pickled sliced jalapeño

Jeffrey Morgenthaler's Homemade Grenadine

Combine 2 cups (473ml) 100% pomegranate juice, 2 cups (400g) sugar, and 2fl oz (60ml) pomegranate molasses in a saucepan and stir over medium heat until the sugar is fully dissolved. Turn off the heat, stir in 1 teaspoon (5ml) orange blossom water and allow to cool before bottling.

The Tequila Sunrise is known primarily as a 1970s concoction of orange juice, tequila, and grenadine. However, there is an older version that is more enjoyable. In the 1930s, Gene Sulit created the original Tequila Sunrise at the Arizona Biltmore Hotel in Phoenix, Arizona. This version called for tequila, crème de cassis, lime juice, and soda water. In 2021, the drink was modified again by barman and cocktail Youtuber Anders Erickson, giving it more depth and balance.

Modified "Original" Tequila Sunrise

SERVES 1

- **1½fl oz (45ml) blanco or reposado tequila**
- **½fl oz (15ml) crème de cassis**
- **½fl oz (15ml) homemade grenadine (*see above*)**
- **¾fl oz (22ml) fresh lime juice**
- **1 dash Angostura bitters**
- **soda water, to top**

To garnish:

- **lime wheel**
- **maraschino cherry**

Combine all ingredients except for the soda water in a cocktail shaker with ice. Shake until cold and strain into a Collins glass with fresh ice and top with soda water. Garnish with a lime wheel and a cherry and serve with a straw.

Victor Bergeron, known more famously as Trader Vic, created the El Diablo by adapting a rum cocktail recipe he found in Hyman Gale and Gerald F. Marco's *The How and When* book from 1940. Originally named Mexican El Diablo, Trader Vic published his recipe for the first time in his 1946 book, *Trader Vic's Book of Food & Drink*. By 1968, Trader Vic had shortened its name to El Diablo and it became the classic drink we know today.

El Diablo

Combine the tequila, crème de cassis, and lime juice in a cocktail shaker with ice. Shake until chilled and strain into a Collins glass with fresh ice. Top with ginger beer and garnish with a lime wedge.

SERVES 1

1½fl oz (45ml) reposado tequila

½fl oz (15ml) crème de cassis

½fl oz (15ml) lime juice

ginger beer, to top

To garnish:
lime wedge

As with most highball-style drinks, the exact origin of the Ranch Water is hard to pin down. It is certain, though, that the drink in its various forms was floating around Texas for a couple of decades before its debut in the late 1990s. Austin-based chef and restaurateur, Kevin Williamson, claimed that Ranch Water appeared for the first time on his Ranch 616 restaurant menu in 1998. However, Ranch 616 did not open its doors until the summer of 1999. It is also worth noting that Williamson's Ranch Water was essentially a Margarita on the rocks made with tequila, Cointreau, and lime juice served in a Collins glass with a bottle of Topo Chico sparkling mineral water on the side. In 2010, a version of Williamson's four-ingredient Ranch Water popped up on the menu of the White Buffalo Bar at the Gage Hotel in Marathon, Texas, but with the drink fully assembled. By 2016, most Ranch Water recipes had dropped the Cointreau to list just three ingredients.

Ranch Water

SERVES 1

1½fl oz (45ml) blanco tequila

½fl oz (15ml) lime juice

sparkling water, to top

To garnish:
lime wedge

Combine all ingredients in a highball or Collins glass over ice. Stir briefly to mix and garnish.

The Blanco Ramos is a tequila variation on the New Orleans cocktail, the Ramos Gin Fizz. Spirits consultant Danny Ronen created the Blanco Ramos in the summer of 2017 while he was guest bartending at Cane & Table bar in New Orleans' French Quarter. According to Ronen, the inclusion of green strawberry bitters and the strawberry garnish give the drink an aroma that is both unique and wonderful.

Blanco Ramos

Combine all ingredients except for the soda water in a cocktail shaker without ice. Dry shake vigorously for at least 10 seconds and carefully open the shaker. Add ice and shake again for about 15 seconds. Strain into a chilled Collins glass and slowly top up with soda water to allow an egg white head to form on top.

For the garnish, take a small to medium sized strawberry and make thin parallel slices from just below the stem to the end of the strawberry. Gently push down on the strawberry to fan the slices out, skewer with a cocktail pick and balance the pick across the rim of the glass.

SERVES 1

2fl oz (60ml) blanco tequila

¾fl oz (22ml) simple syrup

½fl oz (15ml) heavy (double) cream

½fl oz (15ml) lemon juice

½fl oz (15ml) lime juice

2 dashes green strawberry bitters (optional)

2 dashes orange flower water

1 egg white

soda water, to top

To garnish

red or green strawberry

cocktail pick

John Bernard created Something Tequila at his bar, the Porco Lounge & Tiki Room in Cleveland, Ohio. The drink was inspired by a guest who came into the bar and asked if they made Margaritas or "something tequila?" Bernard began with the idea of a classic Rum Barrel—a cocktail filled with a bit of everything that is still very drinkable—and, of course, added tequila.

Something Tequila

SERVES 1

3fl oz (90ml) añejo tequila

1fl oz (30ml) simple syrup

1fl oz (30ml) pineapple juice

1fl oz (30ml) orange juice

1fl oz (30ml) lime juice

½fl oz (15ml) passion fruit syrup

To garnish:
mint

orange slice

lime slice

pineapple frond

Combine all the ingredients with ice in a cocktail shaker. Shake until chilled and open pour (without a strainer) into a tiki mug or Collins glass. Garnish as you like with a sprig of mint, slices of citrus, pineapple frond or any other fun garnish.

GLOSSARY

Abocante One of four allowable mellowing agents defined in the NOM for tequila. These include caramel coloring, oak extract, glycerine, and sugar syrup. These can be used in most classes and categories of tequila up to 5g/liter by dry weight.

Añejo The Spanish word for aged; in the tequila world, a class of tequilas that have been rested in oak barrels for a minimum of one year and maximum of three years.

Autoclave A pressurized stainless steel tube that is used for cooking agave piñas. Because the autoclave is pressurized it can significantly reduce the amount of time needed to cook the agaves.

Baijiu A spirit style that originated in China. This spirit is made by steaming grains, such as sorghum, wheat, rice, or corn and inoculating it with a mixture of mold and yeast called qu (chew) that breaks the starches into fermentable sugars. Once fermented the grains are packed into a still and steam is pumped in, to strip the alcohol out of the mixture.

Blanco The Spanish word for white; in the tequila world blanco refers to unaged tequila or tequila that has been rested in oak for less than two months.

Brix A measurement of the percentage of dissolved sugar in a liquid. Brix is used by winemakers and distillers as a way to estimate the amount of alcohol their yeast should be able to produce from a given batch of grapes, or agaves.

Clamato A brand name mixture of tomato juice, clam juice, and spices.

Coupage A French wine practice of blending wines from different grapes to create a final product. This practice has been adopted by some tequila makers who will blend separate batches of tequila made with different water sources from different agave fields to create unique flavor profiles.

Cristalino A marketing term that the tequila world has coined for aged tequilas that have been filtered to remove any color from the aging process.

Daisy cocktail A family of cocktails that combine sprit, juice, and liqueurs. Because of the addition of juice, these drinks are usually shaken before being served in the appropriate glass. Daisies are similar to sours, but sours are sweetened with simple syrup rather than a liqueur such as triple sec.

D.O.C. An abbreviation for Denominación de Origen Controlada or denomination of origin. These are legal declarations by the Mexican government that identify goods that are a unique cultural product of Mexico from specific geographic regions. DOCs protect 18 unique products of Mexico including tequila, mezcal, and coffee from Veracruz.

Horno A Spanish word for oven; in the tequila world hornos generally refers to brick or stone, above-ground, steam-fed ovens used to cook piñas.

Mixto A colloquial term used by people in the drinks industry and tequila aficionados to refer to tequilas that were not made from 100% agave. Mixto is not a legally defined term but is commonly used when speaking or writing about tequila made from fermenting a mixture of agave and non-agave based sugars.

NOM An abbreviation for Norma Oficial Mexicana. In Mexico, NOMs define standards for everything from weights, measures, food standards, specifications for regional styles of pottery, and for distilled spirits such as tequila and mezcal.

Orgeat A flavored syrup made from almonds, sugar, and flower waters such as rose water and orange blossom water.

Panela Also known as piloncillo, panela is an unrefined cane sugar popular in Latin America that boils cane juice until the sugars begin to crystalize. Panela is often shaped into bricks, discs, or cones before being sold.

Pechuga The Spanish word referring to a chicken or turkey breast. Pechuga also refers to a practice in Mexico of re-distilling agave spirits with meat, nuts, fruit, and spices to flavor the spirit, similar to how gin is made by redistilling grain spirits with juniper and other botanicals. Because pecugas are more labor intensive and result in a smaller yield, they were traditionally reserved for celebrations or festivals.

Piña A Spanish word for pineapple; in the word of tequila, piña refers to the heart of the agave plant after the leaves (pencas) have been shaved off by the jimador. The pattern of the heart makes it look like a white and green pineapple, hence the name.

Pulque A pre-Columbian beverage native to Mexico made from the fermented nectar of the agave plant. The heart of the agave is carved out and the nectar fills the cavity. Each day the pulquero collects the liquid and allows it to ferment naturally.

Reposado The Spanish word for rested; in the tequila world reposado is a class of tequilas that have been rested in oak containers for a minimum of two months and less than one year.

Reverse osmosis A physical system that separates H_2O water molecules from other larger solids or dissolved molecules in a liquid. Pressure is applied to a liquid and a semipermeable membrane only allows molecules of a certain size to pass through. In distilling, reverse osmosis is commonly used to remove trace amounts of minerals or salts from water before it is used in proofing spirits.

Sal de gusano A savory flavored salt made by roasting moth larva that are commonly found on agave plants, grinding them into a powder and mixing with salt.

Shochu A spirit style that originated in Japan. This spirit is made from fermenting rice or a combination of rice and other ingredients such as barley, buckwheat, sweet potato, or brown sugar. Shochu relies on koji, a type of edible mold that can break down starches into fermentable sugars. After fermentation, traditional shochu is distilled once before being bottled.

Soda Derived from bicarbonate of soda or baking soda, it refers to carbonated water. However, in the US soda has become a colloquial term for sweetened and carbonated soft drinks such has cola or lemonade. Because of this, unless specified as some other adjective like soda water, soda can refer to either carbonated water or a sweetened and carbonated soft drink.

Tahona A large stone or cement wheel used to crush cooked agave to extract the juice from the fibres. Traditionally the wheel was drawn in a circle by a mule or horse and was a technological breakthrough that replaced workers who would crush the cooked agaves with large wooden mallets

Tajín A popular brand of Mexican seasoning made from a mixture of chili pepper, lime, and salt.

INDEX

4 Copas Añejo 67
4 Copas Añejo 110: 67
4 Copas Blanco 66
4 Copas Blanco 110: 66
4 Copas Reposado 67
4 Copas Reposado 110: 67
100% agave tequila 26–7, 35, 42, 55
818 Añejo 69
818 Blanco 68
818 Eight Reserve Añejo 69
818 Reposado 69
1800 Añejo 65
1800 Blanco 64
1800 Cristalino Añejo 65
1800 Milenio Extra Añejo 65
1800 Reposado 64

A

abocantes 25, 47–8, 51, 55
ABV 35, 44, 55, 59
additive-free tequila 28–9
additives 25, 35, 47–8
agave 35. *see also* blue agave
  historic uses for 10, 13–14
  mythical origins 12
  names for 11
  pests & diseases 27
Agave Matchmaker app 28
Agave tequilana. *see* blue agave
Agavoni 180
aging 46–7, 56–7
Albino, Vicente 16
alcohol by volume 35, 44, 55, 59
alembic pot still 11, 17
añejo tequila 25, 56
angel's share 46
ArteNOM 1123 Blanco Histórico 70
ArteNOM 1146 Añejo 71
ArteNOM 1414 Reposado 72
ArteNOM 1579 Blanco 73
Astral Reposado 74
Austin, Ken 75, 165
authorized producers 53
autoclaves 39–40, 50
Avión 194
Avión Reposado 75
Avión Reserva 44 Extra Añejo 75
Aztecs 10, 11, 12

B

barrels 46–7, 48
bat friendly agave 38
Bergeron, Victor 209
Bermejo, Julio 183, 194
Bernard, John 214
Betts, Richard 74, 133
Blanco Ramos 213
blanco tequila 25, 56
Bloody Maria 205
blue agave 7, 23, 35
  growing & harvesting 35–8, 50
  life cycle of 36–7
  nocturnal cycle 38
  pests & diseases 27, 38
bottle labels 52–9
bottling 49, 51
brand names 53. *see also* individual names
Brass, Eric 168

C

Cabo Wabo Blanco 76
Cabo Wabo Reposado 76
Café Royale, London 21, 176, 190, 201
Calirosa Blanco 77
Calle 23 Blanco 78
Calle 23 Reposado 78
Camarena, Alan 123
Camarena, Carlos 116, 146, 159, 163
Camarena family 79, 116, 123, 146, 163
Camarena, Felipe 73, 116, 123, 150, 163, 170
Camarena, Jenny 116, 163
caramel colouring 47–8, 51
Casa Cuervo 64–5, 98, 127, 156
Casa Dragones Añejo 81
Casa Dragones Blanco 80
Casa Dragones Joven 81
Casa Dragones Reposado 81
Casamigos Añejo 83
Casamigos Blanco 82
Casamigos Cristalino Reposado 83
Casamigos Reposado 83
Cascahuín Blanco 84
Cascahuín Tahona Blanco 84
Cazadores Añejo 85
Cazadores Reposado 85
Cazcanes No. 7 Blanco 86
Cazcanes No. 7 Reposado 87
Cazcanes No. 9 Blanco 87
Cazcanes No. 10 Blanco Still Strength 87
Cedano, Marco 168
Cedano, Rodrigo 168
Chicago World's Fair, 1893 18
Chinaco Añejo 89
Chinaco Añejo Ultra Cristalino 89
Chinaco Blanco 88
Chinaco Reposado 89
Cimarron Blanco 90
Cimarron Reposado 90
Clase Azul Reposado 91
cocktails 174–5
  Agavoni 180
  Blanco Ramos 213
  Bloody Maria 205
  Corpse Reviver Numero Dos 198
  Distrito Federal 194
  El Diablo 209
  Frozen Margarita 22, 188
  Margarita 176
  Mexican Firing Squad 179
  Modified "Original" Tequila Sunrise 206
  Paloma 202
  Picador 21, 190
  Ranch Water 210
  Siesta 193
  Tequila Bee's Knees 184
  Tequila Old Fashioned 187
  Tommy's Margarita 183
  Toreador '25: 201
  White Dragon 197
Código 1530 Añejo 93
Código 1530 Blanco 92
Código 1530 Origen Extra Añejo 93
Código 1530 Rosa Blanco 93
column stills 44, 45–6, 51
Consejo Regulador Del Tequila (CRT) 25, 26, 28–9, 30, 48, 54, 59
Corazón Single Estate Añejo 95
Corazón Single Estate Blanco 94
Corazón Single Estate Extra Añejo 95
Corazón Single Estate Reposado 95
Coronado, Andy 135
Corpse Reviver Numero Dos 198
Corralejo Añejo 97
Corralejo Extra Añejo 97
Corralejo Reposado 97
Corralejo Silver 96
Cortés, Hernán 10, 11
Craddock, Harry 198
cristalino tequila 57
Cuervo family 114, 132, 156
  Casa Cuervo 64–5, 98, 127, 156
Cuervo, Jorge Antonio 114
Cuervo, Jorge Salles 113, 114
Cuervo, José Antonio de 14–15
Cuervo, José Maria 15, 16, 17
Cuervo, José Prudencio de 15
Cuervo Tradicional Añejo 99
Cuervo Tradicional Blanco 98
Cuervo Tradicional Cristalino Reposado 99
Cuervo Tradicional Reposado 99
Cutwater Añejo 101
Cutwater Blanco 100
Cutwater Extra Añejo 101
Cutwater Reposado 101

D

daisy cocktails 21, 176
De Anda Orozco family 66, 103
Decobecq, Sophie 78
DeLeón Añejo 102
DeLeón Reposado 102
Delgado Corona, Javier 113
Denomination of Origin 23–4, 25, 26, 32–3, 54
Denton, Robert 116
Dichter, Kenny 75
diffusers 40, 50
distillation 44–6, 51
  changes in 17
  history of 11–12, 17, 44–5
Distrito Federal 194

Divertido Blanco 103
Divertido Reposado 103
Don Fulano Añejo 105
Don Fulano Blanco 104
Don Fulano Blanco Fuerte 104
Don Fulano Imperial Extra Añejo 105
Don Fulano Reposado 105
Don Julio 70 Cristalino Añejo 107
Don Julio 1942 Extra Añejo 107
Don Julio Añejo 107
Don Julio Blanco 106
Don Julio Reposado 106
Dulce Vida Organic 100 Proof Blanco 108
Dulce Vida Organic 100 Proof Extra Añejo 109
Dulce Vida Organic 100 Proof Reposado 109
Dulce Vida Organic Blanco 108
Dulce Vida Organic Reposado 109

E

Edwards, Colin & Chris 86
Egyptian mill. *see tahonas*
El Ateo Blanco 110
El Ateo Reposado 110
El Diablo 209
El Mayor Añejo 112
El Mayor Blanco 111
El Mayor Cristalino Añejo 112
El Mayor Reposado 111
El Mayor Rosado Reposado 112
El Tequileño (100% Agave) Cristalino Reposado 115
El Tequileño (100% Agave) Platinum Still Strength 114
El Tequileño (100% Agave) Reposado Gran Reserva 115
El Tequileño (100% Agave) Reposado Rare 115
El Tequileño Blanco 113
El Tequileño Reposado 113
El Tesoro Añejo 116
El Tesoro Blanco 116
El Viejito Plata 42: 117
El Viejito Reposado 117
English, Camper 202
Erickson, Anders 206
Espolòn Añejo 119
Espolòn Blanco 118
Espolòn Cristalino Añejo 119
Espolòn Reposado 119
Esquire magazine 21–2, 132, 176
estates 58
Estes, Tomas 146
evaporation 46
extra añejo tequila 57
extraction 40–2, 50

F

Fagnan, Jenna 165
Familia Camarena Reposado 79
fermentation 42–4, 50
Flores, Jesús 17–18
Fonseca, Enrique 71, 90, 104, 121, 137, 154, 166
Fortaleza Blanco 120
Fortaleza Reposado 120
Frozen Margarita 22, 188
Fuenteseca Cosecha 2018 Blanco 122
Fuenteseca Reserva 5 Years Extra Añejo 122

G

G4 Blanco 123
G4 Extra Añejo 124
G4 High Proof Blanco 124
G4 Reposado 124
Gallardo family 171
Gallardo, Lázaro 125, 158
Gallardo, Luciano 125
Gallardo, Santiago Cortina 171
Gerber, Rande 82
'gluten-free' tequila 28
glycerin 48, 51, 58
gold tequila 56
González Díaz Lombardo, Guillermo 24–5, 88
Gonzalez family 111, 136
González-Frausto Estrada, Julio 106, 136
Gonzalez, Graciela 111
González Nieves, Bertha 80
Gonzalez Vargas, Ignacio 160
Gran Centenario Cristalino Añejo 126
Gran Centenario Leyenda Extra Añejo 126
Gran Centenario Plata 125
Gran Centenario Reposado 126
Gran Coramino Añejo 127
Gran Coramino Cristalino Reposado 127
Guindi, Moises 144

H

Hacienda Corralejo 96
Hacienda Cuisillos 12–13
Hagar, Sammy 76
Hart, Kevin 127
harvesting 37–8, 50
Hennessy, Moët 171
Hernandez, Albert 188
Hernandez Barba, Pedro 161
Hernández, Jesús 148
Herradura 19
Herradura Añejo 129
Herradura Legend Añejo 129
Herradura Reposado 128
Herradura Selección Suprema Extra Añejo 129
Hess, Robert 180
Heuser, Bastian 180
high proof tequila 59
history of tequila 10, 30–1
  16th century 11–12, 14
  17th century 13–15
  18th century 14–15
  19th century 16–18
  20th century 19–23, 26, 27
  21st century 27–8
  additive-free tequila 28–9
  changes in production 17
  classification 25, 26–8, 32–3, 56–7
  cocktails boost sales 21–3
  Consejo Regulador Del Tequila (CRT) 25, 26, 28–9
  Denomination of Origin 23–4, 25, 26, 32–3, 54
  disease and weather, impact of 27
  Don Pedro Sánchez de Tagle 12–13
  economic depression 19
  exports increase 17–18, 26
  legislation 20–1, 23, 25, 26, 32–3
  Norma Oficial Mexicana 25, 26, 32–3, 35
  Nueva Galicia 13–14
  prohibition 14–15, 19
  regulation 23–4, 25, 26, 28–9, 32–3, 35
  sugar content 21, 23, 26, 51
  tequila emerges 16–17
  trade agreements 26
  vino de coco 11–12, 14
  vino de mezcal 13–15, 17
  World War II 19–20
Hocking, Brent 102
Hornitos Plata 130
hornos (ovens) 39, 50
hydrolysis 38–40, 50

I

inulin 37, 38–40

J

Jabir ibn Hayyan 11
JAJA Reposado 131
Jalisco 20, 21, 23, 25, 27, 32–3
  regions of 23–4, 62
jimadors (harvesters) 37–8
Jiménez Lazcarro, Francisco 86
Jose Cuervo 21–2
Jose Cuervo Especial Silver 132
Juarez, Pedro 144

K

Komos Añejo Cristalino 134
Komos Añejo Reserva 134
Komos Extra Añejo 134
Komos Reposado Rosa 133
kosher tequila 58

L

La Gonzaleña distillery 24
La Gritona Reposado 135
La Rojeña 16–17
labels 52–9
LALO Blanco 136
Lapis Platinum 137
Lapis Reposado 137
Lázaro de Arregui, Domingo: *Descripción de la Nueva Galicia* 13–14
leaves. *see pencas*
Levine, Adam 77

Linnaeus, Carl 11
Lomeli, Arturo 91
López, Aurelio 128
López family 165
López, Félix 128, 158
lot/batch numbers 59
Lustig, Jacob 70, 121
Lux, Paul 111

M

Maestro Dobel 50 Cristalino Extra Añejo 140
Maestro Dobel Añejo 140
Maestro Dobel Blanco 138
Maestro Dobel Diamante Cristalino Reposado 139
Maestro Dobel Humito Smoked Silver 139
Maestro Dobel Pavito Blanco 139
Maestro Dobel Reposado 140
maguey 11
Marchese, Joe 133
Margarita 21–2, 176
Martinez, Mariano 188
Masso, Dré 148
maturation 46–7, 51
Mayahuel, Goddess 12
Mayenda Blanco 141
Mayenda Reposado Double Cask 141
McGarry, Jack 205
Meehan, Jim 197
Meldman, Mike 82
Melendrez, Sebastian 66
mellowing agents. *see abocantes*
Mendoza, Sergio 104
mexcatl 11
Mexican Firing Squad 179
Mexico. *see also* history of tequila
  legislation 20–1, 23, 25, 26, 32–3
  prohibition 14–15, 19
  Revolution 19
  Spanish conquest, 1519: 10
  tequila emerges 16–17
  trade agreements 26
  vino de coco 11–12, 14
  vino de mezcal 13–15, 17
  World War II 19–20
mezcal 11
mezcal de Tequila 16–17, 31
miel amarga (bitter honey) 39–40
Mijenta Blanco 142
Mijenta Cristalino Añejo Gran Reserva 143
Mijenta Cristalino Reposado 143
Mijenta Reposado 143
Milagro Añejo 145
Milagro Cristalino Añejo 145
Milagro Reposado 145
Milagro Silver 145
mills
  roller mills 41, 42, 50
  screw mills 41–2
  tahonas 40–1, 50, 58
Miranda, Hector Galindo 66
mixtos 26–7, 42, 55
Modified "Original" Tequila Sunrise 206
Morgenthaler, Jeffrey 206
must 14, 44–6, 50–1

N

NOM Number 54
Norma Oficial Mexicana 25, 26
North American Free Trade Agreement 26
Nueva Galicia 13–14
Núñez, Juan Eduardo 117

O

oak extract 48, 51
Ocho Añejo 147
Ocho Extra Añejo 2015 Loma Alta 147
Ocho Plata 146
Ocho Reposado 147
Olmeca Altos Plata 148
Olmeca Altos Reposado 148
organic tequila 58
Oropeza, Cirilo 118

P

Pall, Alex 131
Paloma 202
Partida family 66, 103
Partida, Iliana 66, 103
Partida Reserva Blanco 149
Partida Reserva Reposado 149
Partida, Sofia 149
Pasote Añejo 151
Pasote Blanco 150
Pasote Reposado 151
Pasote Still Strength Blanco 151
Patrón Blanco 152
Patrón Reposado 152
pencas 37
Picador 21, 190
piñas 38–42
Pittman, Robert 80
Plascencia, Raul 94, 118
pot stills 44, 45, 51
premium tequila 59
Prinsloo, Behati 77
production 35, 50–1
  additives & *abocantes* 47–8, 51
  distillation 44–6, 51
  extraction 40–2, 50
  fermentation 42–4, 50
  growing & harvesting 35–8, 50
  hydrolysis 38–40, 50
  maturation 46–7, 51
  proofing & bottling 49, 51, 59
proofing 49, 51, 59
Pueblo Viejo Blanco 153
Pueblo Viejo Reposado 153
Purasangre Añejo 155
Purasangre Blanco 154
Purasangre Blanco Fuerte 154
Purasangre Reposado 155
Purasangre Reserva 5 Year Extra Añejo 155

R

Ranch Water 210
Real family 77
Reid, Nick 168
reposado tequila 25, 56
Reserva de la Familia Cristalino Añejo 157
Reserva de la Familia Extra Añejo 157
Reserva de la Familia Platino 156
Reserva de la Familia Reposado 157
Richards, Keith 23
Rodriguez Carballido, David 136
Rodriguez Moreno, Leonardo 96
Rojo, Karina 117
roller mills 41, 42, 50
Rolling Stones 22–3
Román, Jesús López 153
Romero, Ana Maria 142
Ronen, Danny 213
  Something Tequila 214
rosa tequila 57
Rosales family 84

S

Salazar, Joséfa 128
Sánchez de Tagle, Don Pedro 12–13
Sanschagrin, Grover & Scarlet 28–9
Santillán, José 86
Sauza, Cenobio 17–18, 31, 120, 130, 158, 167
Sauza, Eladio 158, 167
Sauza family 167
Sauza, Francisco Javier 24, 120, 130, 167
Sauza, Guillermo Erickson 120
Sauza Hacienda Silver 158
The Savoy Hotel 198
Schneeweiss, Danny 144
screw mills 41–2
Sebastiani family 150
Shansby, J. Gary 149
Sherry, Jimmy 168
Siembra Alteño Blanco 159
Siesta 193
Siete Leguas 40
Siete Leguas Añejo 160
Siete Leguas Blanco 160
Smith, Marilyn 116
Snyder, Ron 92
Sokol, Lance 161
Something Tequila 214
Sorenson, Richard 108
Spain: conquest of Mexico, 1519 10
Spiewak, Laurence 161
St Louis World's Fair, 1904 18
stills 44, 45–6, 51
  alembic pot still 11, 17
  column stills 44, 45–6, 51
  Filipino-style 11–12, 14
Stipe, Katie 193
Strait, George 92
Suerte Añejo 162
Suerte Blanco 161
Suerte Reposado 162
Suerte Still Strength Blanco 162

sugar content 21, 23, 26, 51
Sulit, Jean 206
Suro, David 159

T

Taberna de Cuervo 15–16
Taggart. Drew 131
tahonas (mill stones) 40–1, 50, 58
Tamaulipas 23–5
Tapatio Añejo 164
Tapatio Blanco 163
Tapatio Blanco 110: 164
Tapatio Reposado 164
Tarling, William T. 21, 176, 190, 201
Tebele, Maurice & Elliot 131
Tello, Antonio de 14
tequila 55. *see also* individual brands
  brand variety 6, 7
  classification 25, 26–8, 32–3, 56–7
  marketing terms 58–9
  popularity of 6
  production regions 23–4, 62
  sugar content 26, 35, 42
Tequila Bee's Knees 184
Tequila Matchmaker app 28
Tequila Old Fashioned 187
Tequila Sunrise 22–3, 132, 206
Tequila (village) 14–17, 30
Teremana Blanco 165
Teremana Reposado 165
terroir 70, 121, 146, 159
Tommy's Margarita 183
Toreador '25: 201
Trader Vic 209
Tres Cuatro y Cinco Extra Añejo 166
Tres Generaciones Plata 167
Tres Generaciones Reposado 167
Tromba Añejo 169
Tromba Cedano Reposado 169
Tromba Reposado 168
Tromba XA Extra Añejo 169

V

Vigneaux, Ernest 17
Villa, Francisco 19
Villalobos, Luis Ángel 110
Villarreal, Carmen 94, 153
vinazas 45, 46
vino de coco 11–12, 14
vino de mezcal 13–15, 17
Vivanco family 72
Volans Blanco 170
Volans Still Strength Blanco 170
Volcan de mi Tierra Blanco 171

W

White Dragon 197
Williamson, Kevin 210

Y

yeast 43–4, 50, 58

Z

Zandona, Tia 201, 205

PICTURE CREDITS

Mitchell Beazley would like to thank all the distilleries, producers and their agents who have kindly helped us by providing images for publication in this book.

Courtesy Cuervo: 15 (& 8cr); Proximo Spirits: 16 (& 8ac), 64-65, 98-99, 125-27, 131, 132, 138-140, 156-57; Courtesy La Gonzaleña 24, 88-89 (& 60cr); Tequila Los Abuelos SA de CV 26, 120; Tequila Tapatio, photo Gabriela Flores Camarena 43, 44 (& 8bc), 163-64;Verde Tequila 66-67, 103 (& 60ac); 818 Tequila 68-69; Terranova Spirits: Tequila ArteNOM 70-73, Tequila Cimarron 90, Tequila Fuenteseca 121-22, Tequila Lapis 137, Tequila Purasangre 154-55; Tres Cuatro y Cinco Tequila 166; © 2026 Diageo. All rights reserved. Used by permission 74, 82-83, 102, 106-107; Courtesy Pernod Ricard 75, 92-93, 148; Calirosa Tequila 77; Calle 23 Tequila 78; Photograph from the Familia Camarena Collection © E. & J. Gallo Winery 79; Tequila Casa Dragones 80-81; Cascahuin 84; Cazcanes Tequila 86-87; Clase Azul Mexico 91; Sazerac 94-95; Corralejo Tequila/Infinium Spirits 96-97; Cutwater Spirits 100-101; Don Fulano Tequila 104-105; Dulce Vida Tequila 108-109; Courtesy of PKGD Group 110, 117 (& 60bl), 123-24; Luxco, Inc 111-12; El Tequileño 113-15; Suntory Global Spirits 116, 130, 158, 167; Campari Group 118-19; The Herradura trademarks appear courtesy of Brown-Forman Corporation. HERRADURA is a registered trademark of Brown-Forman Corporation 128-29; Photographs from the Casa Komos © E. & J. Gallo Winery 133-34; La Gritona Tequila LLC. Photo Nicola Parisi 135 (& 60ar); Courtesy LALO Spirits 136; Mijenta 142-43; © 2019 William Grant & Sons Brands Limited. All rights reserved. Photographs are owned by William Grant & Sons Brands Limited and used under non-exclusive licence 144-45; Tequila Ocho 146-47 (& 60cl); Tequila Partida team 149; Images provided by Maguey Spirits, brand owner of Pasote Tequila 150-51 (& 60c); Pueblo Viejo 153; Courtesy Siembra Alteño. Photo Gilberto Hernández 159 (& 60al); Suerte Tequila 161-62 (& 60br); Teremana 165; Tromba 168-69 (& 60bc); Volans Spirits 170; Volcan de Mi Terra 171.

Additional images:
Courtesy Agave Matchmaker 48; Alamy Stock Photo: Abriel Trujillo/dpa/Alamy Live News 49, Album 12a, Brian Overcast 23, 40, The History Collection 10, Hugh Mitton 47 (& 8ar), Jorge Garrido 2 (& 8cl); Photo Researchers/ Science History Images 11, The Picture Collection 12b, q77photo 52, Quagga Media 14, Retro AdArchives, with the permission of Cuervo 22 (& 8bl); Richard Ellis 41, SBS Eclectic Images 35, World History Archive 19; Getty Images: DEA/Gianni Dagli Orti 13 (& 8al), Justin Sullivan 25, Mauricio Palos/Bloomberg via Getty Images 20, The Werner Company/Field Museum Library 18; iStock: José de Jesus Churion 7, Wirestock 34 (& 8c); Shutterstock: Jesus Cervantes 42, José de Jesus Churión 27, 37 (& 8br), 38, Kit Leong 39.

Cristian Barnett for Octopus Publishing Group: 4, 172-215

Key: a above, b below, c centre, l left, r right

ACKNOWLEDGEMENTS

I would like to thank a number of people without whose support and inspiration this book would not have been possible. I'd like to begin with some thanks for my friend David T. Smith, who helped me work through a sticking point in the writing process. I'd also like to thank Mike Morales, Bryce Taylor, Grover Sanschagrin, and Rabbi Sholom Tendler for helping provide technical details about some aspects of tequila production. David Dinius, Matt Metras, and Bryce also helped me source a tequila sample that had alluded me. Lou Bank, Salvador Periban, DTS, Sara L. Smith, Big T, Queenie, Hartley, and Mom for providing your support, encouragement, and design perspectives. Danny Ronen, Greg Titian, and Anders Erickson for cocktail inspiration. To my brother Joshua Gonzales and friend Reece Sims for helping me open my thinking on *cristalinos*. And, thank you to Octopus Publishing Group for working with me again—and, in particular, Jeannie Stanley and the rest of the team for making the process so smooth, collecting bottle images, editing my prose, and making this book a reality.

I would also like to thank all of the distillers and people involved in the process of creating tequila. Your passion, dedication, and spirit are inspiring. Also, to the industry people and brands that helped me source or directly supplied tasting samples, including Virginia Miller, Rachel Dorcy, Monique Houston, Sarah Nagel Sisisky, Shawn Miller, Henry Preiss, Jacob Lustig, Andre Espinoza, Sacha Bell, Jennifer Fruzzetti, and many others.

And, in particular, I would like to thank four tequila bars that allowed me to taste brands and expressions I was not able to get directly from the producers. Barrio in San Francisco, California, is a fun restaurant and agave bar overlooking the San Francisco Bay from Ghirardelli Square that has the feel of a swim up bar but without the pool. Michael Carlisi oversees its bar program and, over four years, it has created a tasty menu using fresh California ingredients inspired by Latin cuisine. Cavaña bar and restaurant, also in San Francisco, is run by managing partner Anthony Parks, beverage director Emilio Salehi, and bar manager Miguel Salehi. Together they have built a welcoming rooftop bar in Mission Bay that offers music, dancing, a menu of Pan-Latin cuisine and cocktails created from the spirits of Latin American including tequila, mezcal, pisco, and cachaça. Mayahuel in downtown Sacramento, California, is an expansive restaurant and bar that celebrates the food, drinks, art, and music of Mexico. Owner Ernesto Delgado and bar manager Angela González have curated a large collection of tequilas and offer tastings to help people discover some of Mexico's great spirits. And lastly, Midtown's Cantina Alley, also in Sacramento. Since 2017, it has offered an authentic cantina experience with Mexican street foods and a great cocktail program designed by bar manager Oscar Escobar.

Lastly, I would like to thank my amazing wife Tia for her support, and encouragement, for helping to test and refine cocktail recipes, and for keeping our boys busy while I tasted and wrote about tequila. I want to thank my boys Giorgio and Elio who gave me the space to work even they wanted my attention. Without all of their help and sacrifice this could not have happened.

For Mom and Dad

First published in Great Britain in 2026 by Mitchell Beazley, an imprint of
Octopus Publishing Group Ltd
Carmelite House
50 Victoria Embankment
London EC4Y 0DZ
www.octopusbooks.co.uk

An Hachette UK Company
www.hachette.co.uk

The authorized representative in the EEA is Hachette Ireland, 8 Castlecourt Centre, Dublin 15, D15 XTP3, Ireland (email: info@hbgi.ie)

Distributed in the US by Hachette Book Group
1290 Avenue of the Americas,
4th and 5th Floors, New York, NY 10104

Distributed in Canada by Canadian Manda Group
664 Annette Sreet, Toronto, Ontario, Canada M6S 2C8

ISBN 978-1-84091-983-7
eISBN 978-1-84091-984-4

A CIP catalogue record for this book is available from the British Library.

Printed and bound in China

10 9 8 7 6 5 4 3 2 1

Commissioning Editor: Jeannie Stanley
Senior Editor: Pauline Bache
Editor: Rosie Hilton
Copy editor: Molly Price
Art Director: Juliette Norsworthy
Designer: Geoff Fennell
Cover design: Mominah Aslam
Special Photography: Cristian Barnett
Food and props stylist: Emily Ezekiel
Picture Research Manager: Jen Veall
Picture Researcher: Giulia Hetherington
Assistant Production Manager: Lisa Pinnell